Mountains in Tokyo

	elevation (m)
Mt. Kumotori	2017
Mt. Toridani	1718
Mt. Mito	1531
Mt. Kawanori	1363
Mt. Otake	1266
Minami-Iwoto Isl.	916
Mt. Jimba	855
Mt. Mishi (Hachijo-Fuji) [Hachijojima Isl.]	854
Mt. Oyama [Mikurajima Isl.]	851
Mt. Sakakigamine [Kita-Iwoto Isl.]	792
Mt. Oyama [Miyakejima Isl.]	775
Mt. Mihara (Mihara-shinzan) [Oshima Isl.]	758
Mt. Takao	599
Mt. Tenjo [Kozushima Isl.]	572
Mt. Miyatsuka [Toshima Isl.]	508
Mt. Chibusa [Hahajima Isl.]	463
Mt. Iwo [Torishima Isl.]	394
Mt. Chuo [Chichijima Isl.]	320
Mt. Suribachi (Mt. Pipe) [Iwoto Isl.]	170

Based on Geographical Survey Institute website
"Mountains in Tokyo" (in Japanese)

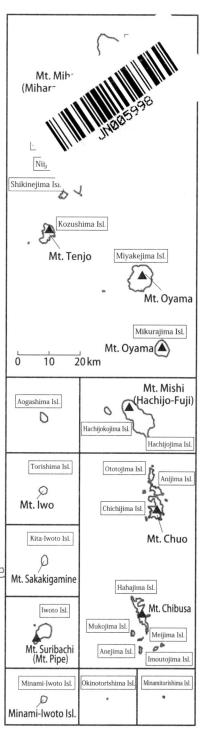

Geography
of
Tokyo

東京地理入門

edited by

Toshio Kikuchi
Hiroshi Matsuyama
Lidia Sasaki
Eranga Ranaweerage

Asakura Publishing

Editors

Toshio Kikuchi	Tokyo Metropolitan University
Hiroshi Matsuyama	Tokyo Metropolitan University
Lidia Sasaki	Tokyo Metropolitan University
Eranga Ranaweerage	Tokyo Metropolitan University

Contributors

Hiroshi Matsuyama	Tokyo Metropolitan University
Takehiko Suzuki	Tokyo Metropolitan University
Hideo Takahashi	Tokyo Metropolitan University
Hiroshi Takahashi	Tokyo Metropolitan University
Sadao Takaoka	Senshu University
Tatsuhiro Isogai	Kokushikan University
Kei Ota	Takasaki City University of Economics
Kazuki Ishikawa	Tokyo Metropolitan University
Daichi Nakayama	Tokyo Metropolitan University
Toshio Kikuchi	Tokyo Metropolitan University
Myungjin Hong	Shizuoka Eiwa Gakuin University
Ryo Iizuka	Teikyo University
Yoshiki Wakabayashi	Tokyo Metropolitan University
Ryo Koizumi	Kanagawa University
Hitoshi Miyazawa	Ochanomizu University
Kantaro Takahashi	Akita University
Hitoshi Yagai	Institute of Behavioral Sciences
Naoto Yabe	Tokyo Metropolitan University
Koun Sugimoto	Toyo University
Akira Nakayama	Tokyo Metropolitan University

First published in Japan in 2020 by Asakura Publishing Company, Ltd.
6-29, Shin'Ogawa-machi Shinjuku-ku, Tokyo 162-8707, Japan

Copyright © 2020 edited by Toshio Kikuchi, Hiroshi Matsuyama,
Lidia Sasaki, Eranga Ranaweerage
ISBN 978-4-254-16362-9

All rights reserved. No part of this publication may be reproduced,
stored in a retrieval system, or transmitted in any form or by any means,
electronic, mechanical, photocopying, recording or otherwise,
without prior written permission.

Foreword

Tokyo is a global city, a place where people, goods, capital (money), and information are densely concentrated. At the same time, with the information revolution of the 21st century, we are entering a new borderless era of instant mobility of people, goods, capital (money), and information. Moreover, in continuously expanding Tokyo, various kinds of discrepancies and new issues continue to emerge day by day. In order to solve such issues, it is vital to be able to grasp the real situation, and this is when geographers are called into action.

In this book entitled "Geography of Tokyo", topics of physical geography and human geography are introduced in a balanced, cross-disciplinary manner. Tokyo's panoramic view comes to life based on solid geographic scientific knowledge, introduced in an easy-to understand manner by experts in various fields, all affiliated with Tokyo Metropolitan University.

Besides the introduction and closing chapter, the book consists of 8 chapters. Each includes a main section which is composed of a broad overview of the theme, along with several "Close-up" sections focused on more specific topics. While the chapters are loosely related, they deal with independent topics, so readers can feel free to approach each chapter separately, as suits their needs. The book concentrates a lot of information in this compact format. The authors would be delighted if it succeeds to incite interest in Tokyo's geography, history and culture. We would like to encourage readers to use this book as a field guide and go out in search of adventure. There are so many new things to discover out there!

Released shortly before the 2020 Tokyo Olympic/Paralympic Games, we hope this book may contribute to the re-discovery of Tokyo's many charms.

April 2020

Hiroshi Matsuyama, authors' representative

After the release of this book's Japanese version, Tokyo Olympic and Paralympic Games were postponed to the summer of 2021.

Foreword to the English edition

As long term foreign residents in Tokyo, we are familiar with the challenges that visitors face when confronted with the city's contrasts: its seemingly chaotic urban structure and rich green spaces, the eclectic mix of futuristic architecture standing shoulder-to-shoulder with ancient temples and charming old neighborhoods, the confusing transportation network and the perpetual crowds.

This book, targeting the international students and visitors as well as the city's foreign residents, offers geographical, historical and cultural insights, which facilitate a better understanding of Tokyo's unique features and allows readers a panoramic view of one of the world's most fascinating cities.

The first half of the book introduces the natural geographical aspects of Tokyo while the latter focuses on the cultural and historical ones. The book covers a wide range of topics and each chapter includes several close-ups with relevant case studies and concrete examples to illustrate each topic, making it suitable as a field guide for the leisurely exploration of the metropolis. For example, people may have heard or know that Edo is the former name of Tokyo. In this book, we introduce Edo's culture, food, and holidays to show Edo's influence on Tokyo and provide an enhanced understanding of how it shaped Tokyo's identity as the vibrant and unique megacity of today.

With Tokyo hosting next year's Olympic and Paralympic Games, we look forward to welcoming visitors from all over the world. The book showcases not only the popular forms of urban tourism in the central areas of Tokyo, but also the city's lesser-known regional tourism resources that are yet to be explored by travellers. We hope our book will inspire readers to go out, experience the city's diverse charms and meet its friendly people.

Dr. Lidia Sasaki, editor
Dr. Eranga Ranaweerage, editor

Contents

Chapter 3   Vegetation and Wildlife in Tokyo ---- (Sadao Takaoka) ---- *41*

Chapter 4   Tokyo's Waters and Seas ------- (Hiroshi Matsuyama) ---- *57*

Chapter 5   Tokyo's History and Culture ------- (Toshio Kikuchi) ---- *73*

Conclusion Tokyo's Future: Sustainable Tokyo ---- (Toshio Kikuchi) ---- *137*

Introduction | Discover Tokyo

Tokyo Skytree seen from Sumidagawa Terrace
(photo by Hiroshi Matsuyama in March 2019)

In this chapter, we consider the emergence of Tokyo as a global city on a par with London, Paris and New York, by focusing on different spatial/temporal scales and their importance. We then introduce the city's natural environment, which is the backdrop for the lives of Tokyo's millions of inhabitants.

1. Discover Tokyo from different spatial scales

Tokyo's extent   Let's take a look at the following 3 maps (Fig. 1).   The first one (Fig. 1a), at the scale of 1:5,000,000, shows the whole Japanese archipelago.   On this map, Tokyo is represented as a mere dot.   The next one (Fig. 1b), at the scale of 1:500,000, shows the border line between Tokyo Bay and the land, railways and the road network etc.   The third one (Fig. 1c), at the scale of 1:25,000, zooms in to the area around Shibuya Station and clearly shows details of some buildings.   We can grasp quite a lot of details on this map such as the elevation of Dogenzaka and Miyamasuzaka (34.9 m and 27.6 m, respectively), and

Fig. 1 Three maps showing Tokyo and Shibuya (partially modified after Ref. 1) (a) Map of Japan and surroundings, at the scale of 1:5,000,000, (b) Map at the scale of 1:500,000, (c) Map at the scale of 1:25,000

Shibuya Station squeezed in between, located as its name suggests, at the bottom of the valley.

Incidentally, Shibuya Station is the first one of the Ginza Metro Line, and the trains start from the 3rd level above ground of the station building—a surprising fact if we remember that this is an underground metro line.

It becomes obvious that at different map scales (diverse spatial scales), the way we see Tokyo changes, and the quantity of information we can obtain from the map also differs. So, when talking about Tokyo, what is its spatial extent, and where are its boundaries? For some people, Tokyo proper means the central part of the city, with its 23 wards. For others, Tokyo means the entire expanse of the metropolis. In this case, its boundaries include the Izu and Ogasawara Islands and the western suburbs of the Tama area. Wider even, other people consider the Greater Tokyo Region as encompassing almost entirely Saitama, Chiba and Kanagawa Prefectures, as well as the southern sector of Ibaraki Prefecture, areas which are socio-economically integrated with Tokyo Metropolis (Ref. 2). These "23 wards of Tokyo", "Tokyo Metropolis", and "Greater Tokyo Region" form an overlapping structure similar to Russian dolls, each at their different spatial scales.

The geographical perspective As illustrated in the above example, in geography, the natural environment enabling people's activities on the one hand and the totality of the human-made environment on the other are approached at their respective spatial scales, and the understanding of regional differences is prioritized. In order to solve the problems of our contemporary society and civilization, it is indispensable to focus our scientific approaches at the interface between nature and human society. In this respect, it is necessary to focus on the differences arising from the changes in scale, and to hold a multiscale vision/approach. In addition to the above-mentioned spatial scale, we also need to consider the temporal scale in this case. This is a very useful perspective, which can be helpful when looking at and understanding Tokyo.

2. Tokyo's population and the Kanto Plain nourishing it

Tokyo's population and population density Among the three scales of Tokyo proper, i.e., the 23 wards, Tokyo Metropolis, and the Greater Tokyo Region, the scale of Tokyo Metropolis is the most appropriate for the purposes of this chapter. Tokyo Metropolis consists of the 23 wards, 26 cities, 5 towns and 8 villages. The 23 wards are under metropolitan jurisdiction, but are governed by their respective local assemblies deciding on local matters, so they are special administrative units. Currently, Tokyo is the only metropolis in Japan, so there are only 23 wards of Tokyo, but in the future, with Osaka Prefecture becoming a metropolis, the number of special wards is bound to increase.

As of October 1st 2017, the total area of Tokyo Metropolis was 2,193.96 km^2 and it had a population of 13,754,043 inhabitants (Ref. 3). This results in a population density of 6,269 inhabitants/km^2. If we focus on the 23 wards, with an area of 627.57 km^2 and 9,484,125 inhabitants, the population density is 15,112 inhabitants/km^2.

According to the data of the national census in October 2015, average population density in Japan was 341 inhabitants/km^2, so the difference between this and average densities for Tokyo Metropolis or the 23 wards is remarkable. At the same census, population in Tokyo was 13,513,734 inhabitants, which means that within only 2 years, its population increased by 240,000 people. In the context of general population decline in Japan, this unique trend is characteristic for Tokyo (see Chapter 6).

The Greater Tokyo Region expands radially about 70 km from the center of the city proper and, according to 2007 data, it had a population of 35.3 million people, which translates as one fourth of the total population of Japan (Ref. 2). If we make global comparisons for the same year, Tokyo comes first, with Mexico City

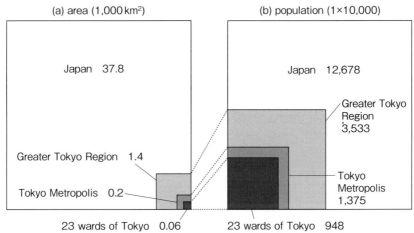

Fig. 2 (a) Area and (b) population of Japan, Greater Tokyo Region, Tokyo Metropolis, and 23 wards of Tokyo (based on Ref. 2-4)

second with 18.7 million inhabitants, and New York third with 18.7 million. Such data are illustrated in Fig. 2, but the question remains: how did it become possible that so many people can live in Tokyo and its environs?

The natural environment of the Kanto Plain   To answer this question, we need to understand the natural environment of the Greater Tokyo Region, especially that of the Kanto Plain. The multi-scale perspective mentioned above becomes essential in this case.

The area of Tokyo Metropolis consists of mountains, plateaus, hills and lowlands (Fig. 3). In the eastern sector, the lowlands created by the Ara and Tone Rivers (before the Edo period) used to suffer from frequent floods, therefore this area was not suitable for habitation. For this reason, the first action taken by Tokugawa Ieyasu, when he established the shogunate here in 1590, was to control the river flows by redirecting the Tone River away from Tokyo Bay towards the Pacific Ocean (Choshi City in Chiba Prefecture, Fig. 4). However, there are suggestions that the real purpose of the redirection of the Tone River was to create a navigation channel, more than to prevent flooding (Ref. 5). Actually, even after the completion of the redirection project of the Tone River, Edo (currently Tokyo) was hit by mud flows following the eruption of Mt. Asama, and flooding continued to occur during Edo period.

Besides water, rivers also transport sediments. Ara, Tone and other rivers flowing through the Kanto Plain deposit such sediments, and as a result, Kanto Plain became the widest plain in Japan. The fact that the plain is a sedimentation area is explained by its continuous subsidence, which occurs in parallel with the rise of mountain ranges west of the Kanto Plain. This is called the movement of the Kanto tectonic basin, and it also explains the creation of the Musashino

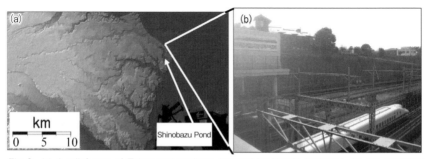

Fig. 3 (a) A relief map of Tokyo and environs (created by Kazuki Ishikawa), (b) the boundary separating the Yamanote Uplands and the Shitamachi Lowlands (JR Nippori Station, photo by Hiroshi Matsuyama in April 2008)

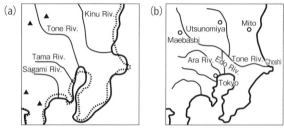

Fig. 4 Tone River before and after its change of direction towards the east (based on Ref. 6)
(a) Before the change: Tone River flowing into Tokyo Bay, (b) after the change: the situation at present

Uplands in the western sector of Tokyo. At present, the subsidence of the Kanto Plain seems to have stopped, but rivers continue to deposit sediments in this area. So, why has the movement of Kanto tectonic basin been occurring?

Plate tectonics　　In order to answer this question, a broader spatial perspective is necessary.

Actually, the Earth's surface is fragmented into more than 10 segments of hard crust, called plates. Depending on the movements of these plates, earthquakes occur and/or mountains are created, and their dynamics is called plate tectonics.

Fig.5 illustrates the location of the four plates in and around Japan. These are the Pacific Plate, the Philippine Sea Plate, the North American Plate and the Eurasian Plate. The first two are oceanic plates, while the last two are continental plates. The oceanic ones are sinking under the continental ones (subduction). The convergence of four plates is a very rare occurrence even at global scale, and it explains why so many earthquakes occur in Japan.

Fig. 5 The situation of tectonic plates in and around Japan (based on Ref. 7)

This means that the subduction of the Pacific and Philippine Sea Plates under the continental plates is directly linked with the movement of Kanto tectonic basin. Actually, the Great Kanto Earthquake in 1923 occurred at the boundary between the Philippine Sea Plate and the North American Plate.

 ## 3. Tokyo's water and history

Urban planning of Edo by Tokugawa Ieyasu and Tokyo as the capital city   With the wide and fertile Kanto Plain as its backdrop, Tokyo had plenty of land for food production as well for people to settle down, so that the Kanto Plain fulfilled all expectations, contributing to the development of the city. In terms of natural conditions and landforms, the location of Tokyo on the Kanto Plain obviously has a huge advantage in comparison with Kyoto, located in a basin surrounded by mountains. According to the Japanese Paleolithic Society (Ref. 8), archeological digs demonstrate that people have been inhabiting the area of western Tokyo around present-day Kodaira and Fuchu Cities since 35,000 years ago. However, there was one limiting factor for increasing numbers of people to concentrate in Edo/Tokyo, which is water.

Concomitant with the project to re-direct the Tone River towards the east (Fig. 4), Tokugawa Ieyasu also built water supply infrastructure, as detailed in Chapter 1 (Close-up: Kanda River and its flow) and Chapter 4. One of the major challenges has been supplying water to the uplands west of the city.

Since Edo's beginning in a wild area with harsh natural conditions up to the present-day Tokyo, Tokugawa Ieyasu's progressive vision of nature transformation and land improvement remains a valuable contribution. At present, the success of such land improvement projects is clearly illustrated by the huge concentration of people in Tokyo.

With a population of more than 1 million inhabitants in the 18th century, the biggest city in the world at that time, Edo became the political center of Japan ever since its establishment by Tokugawa Ieyasu. Later on, following the Meiji Restauration, Edo was renamed Tokyo, and without any legal decision, the national government was established here, with Edo Castle becoming the Imperial Palace. With the legislative power represented by the National Diet, the executive power represented by the Prime Minister, and the judiciary power represented by the Supreme Court of Justice, all concentrated in Tokyo, the city was recognized as the de facto capital of Japan.

Multi-scale temporal perspectives   If we go back to discussing the natural environment, the arrow in Fig. 3(a) points to the Shinobazu Pond, at the foot of the cliff in Ueno Park.   It is easy to imagine that water would spring out in such location, but the author was very surprised to hear that actually the lake is a remnant of the sea.   Such a lake was initially connected with the sea, but gradually sand accumulated and the lake was cut off from the sea due to sea currents and waves.   Although it is difficult to imagine from the present-day situation of Ueno, in the past the sea extended inland into the Kanto plain up to the eastern sector of Saitama Prefecture, because the climate was warmer than today about 7,000 years ago.   In the case of Shinobazu Pond, it is not the classical example of a sea remnant, but it was created by the sand transported by the Ara River which formed a sandbar that blocked the mouth of the rivers flowing at the foot of the uplands.   That's why the outlet of the river gradually turned into a swamp (Ref. 9).

Fig. 6 shows the temperature variation over the past 150,000 years.   About 125,000 years ago, the temperature was similar with the current one, however, about 20,000 years ago, the temperature was about 6°C lower during the Last Glaciation Maximum.   This glaciation ended about 15,000 years ago, and temperatures continued to rise until 7,000 years ago when they were higher than today (Fig. 6).

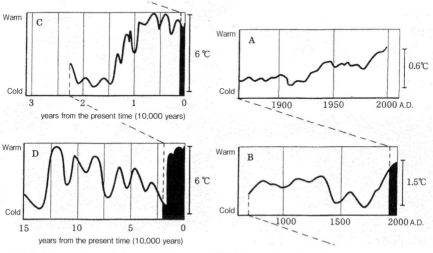

Fig. 6 Temperature variation over the past 150,000 years (modified from Proffessor Emeritus Takehiko Mikami of Tokyo Metropolitan University)

At present, there are warnings about the sea level rise caused by climate change/global warming. However, 7,000 years ago during the warm period, the lowlands in the eastern sector of Tokyo were submerged, and the sea advanced inland covering wide areas of the Kanto Plain (Fig. 1-4b in Chapter 1). Afterwards, the climate cooled and the sea receded, followed by the rivers carrying sediments which they deposited, creating the lowlands of eastern Tokyo. This shows that climate change has had a significant impact on the creation of landforms, as detailed in Chapter 1.

In this introductory chapter, we dealt with various time scales such as 150,000 years interval, 7,000 years ago, and Edo period. We would like to stress that it is important to consider not only the spatial scale, but also the temporal scale when thinking about the origins of natural environment. (Hiroshi Matsuyama)

Chapter 1

Tokyo's Landforms

A cliff line of the east end of Musashino Uplands. JR Keihin Tohoku Line and Shinkansen run by the northeast side of Asukayama Park. (Oji, Kita Ward, photo by Takehiko Suzuki in November 2013)

Tokyo has diverse landforms, from islands to mountains, hills, uplands and lowlands. If we exclude the islands, 1/3 of Tokyo's land area consists of the Kanto Mountains to the west, while the remaining eastern sector is made up of the Kanto Plain. The landforms and geology of the plain are the result of crustal movement, climate change and fluvial and coastal processes.

1.1 Kanto's landforms

The Japanese archipelago is rather mountainous (mountains amount to three-fourths of the territory). In this context, wider plains are favorable landforms for farming and industrial activities, as well as for the location of urban concentrations. As the largest plain in Japan, the Kanto Plain is ideal for the location of the capital city. Was this location planned? Actually, this is not so. If we look back to Japan's history, it was only after the end of the Warrior States area (15–16 century) that it became Japan's center.

Looking at the natural environmental conditions, the current landforms of the Kanto Plain are temporary ones; actually, this was sea area during more than half of the Quaternary geological period (the last 2.6 million years including the present). Even during the warm period before the present one, at the peak of the Last Interglacial Stage (about 125,000 years ago), with climatic conditions similar to the current ones and a similar sea level, most of the Kanto Plain was sea area. The current warm period allowed the remarkable expansion of human population, but Tokyo's development would have not been possible during the previous warm period. Currently, approximately one third of Japan's population is concentrated in the Kanto Plain, but as we mentioned, this was made possible by Kanto's present day landforms.

Landforms of Tokyo and their conditions for the development of a metropolis   Comparing Kanto Plain with other representative plain areas in Japan, we can notice its specific features.   One of these salient features is the expanse of flat landforms of the uplands (Ref. 1).   Compared with the Niigata and Nobi Plains, dominated by lowlands, a specific feature of the Kanto Plain is that it is dominated by uplands.   The most representative are the Musashino, Shimousa and, Omiya Uplands etc. (Fig. 1.1).   Compared with the lowlands, the access to water is difficult and this is why they are not suitable for rice cultivation. For this reason, compared with the lowlands, development of these uplands lagged behind until the Edo period.   On the other hand, they are safe from water-related disasters and the ground is stable and safe.   Furthermore, such uplands are flat, so from the point of view of land use they are convenient.   The Musashino Uplands with their flat landforms lay west of Edo/Tokyo.   During the Meiji, Taisho, Showa and Heisei eras, Tokyo's urban area continued to expand on this flat land.   Furthermore, bordering the uplands towards the west and south, at the contact with the Kanto Mountains area, lay the Tama Hills, where residential land developments such as the Tama New Town later occurred. While the Kanto Mountains area has steep slopes which make development difficult, the west part of the Kanto Plain is suitable for a diversity of land uses.

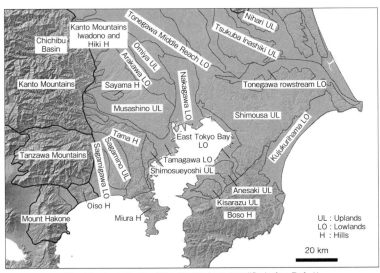

Fig. 1.1   Landforms of the Kanto Area (modified after Ref. 1)

1.2 From mountains to lowlands

Tokyo's mountains: Kanto Mountains   In terms of area, Tokyo ranks 3rd among Japan's smallest administrative units.   However, it is one of the most diverse, its landforms ranging from the volcanic islands, mountains, hills and uplands to lowlands.   Extending longitudinally east–west, one third of Tokyo's area in its west reaches belongs to the Kanto Mountains, called the Okutama Mountains.   The highest peak in the Metropolis can be found at Mt. Kumotori (2,017 m a.s.l.), but the Kanto Mountains have some peaks over 2,500 m, considered "moderately rugged" (Ref. 2).   The geology of the Kanto Mountains includes sedimentary, plutonic, metamorphic rocks etc., but within the metropolitan area dominant are Mesozoic to Paleogene sedimentary rocks, such as limestone, chert, shale, sandstone, all geological formations of the accretionary prism caused by plate motion (Ref. 3).

From hills to uplands, converted *satoyama*   Two thirds of Tokyo's area in the east is part of the Kanto Plain, laying to the east of the Kanto Mountains.   Hilly landforms expand as peninsulas from the mountains towards the east (Fig. 1.2).   Their elevation is low, under 300 m.   Only Sayama Hills exceptionally form an island detached from the mountain area, explained by the

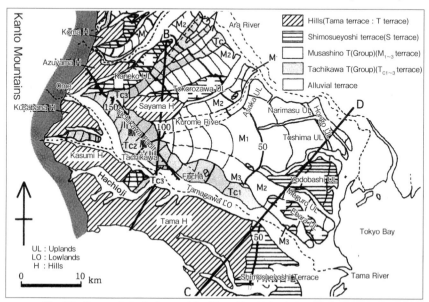

Fig. 1.2   Geomorphological map of the Musashino Uplands (modified after Ref. 1)

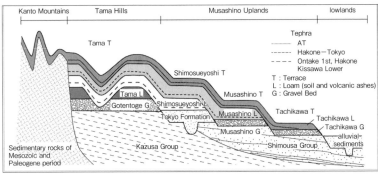

Fig. 1.3 Geological cross-section of the Musashino Uplands

activity of the active Tachikawa Fault which uplifts the northeastern side of the fault (Ref. 1).

The hills in the western area are mainly composed of 3 geological units (Fig. 1.3). The upper one is the Kanto Loam, followed by the older gravel bed originated from the alluvial fans, and the lowest one is the Kazusa Group. The Kanto Loam, composed of the alternation of soils and volcanic ashes, was deposited since 700,000 years ago. Due to erosion, in some areas this unit is missing. The gravels of the alluvial fan are represented, in the case of the Tama Hills, by the Gotentoge Gravel Bed, while in the Sayama Hills these are called the Imokubo Gravel Bed. Such gravels were deposited about 700,000 to 500,000 years ago by the Sagami and Tama Rivers, respectively. At the time, the Sagami River flowed northeast, a totally different course from the current one. For a while, the alluvial fan emerged, forming a river terrace with flat landforms similar to the present day Musashino Uplands, but subsequently due to erosion, it was soon fragmented by valleys and transformed into hilly landforms without flat ground surfaces.

In the past, the valleys offering easy access to water, were used as paddy fields, while the slopes were used for coppice forests to provide charcoal, generating a typical *satoyama* landscape. However, during Japan's rapid economic development era, in many suburban locations large scale conversions were carried out, resulting in the creation of the so-called "bed-towns" such as Tama New Town. In areas of the Tama Hills, where such large scale projects were implemented, the Kanto Loam and the Gotentoge Gravel Bed were cut, in order to level the land. What is left in such areas are the formations of the Kazusa Group. This layer was mainly composed of marine sands and muds deposited on the bottom of the sea floor during the Quaternary geological period, but in the Tama area, closer to the Kanto Mountains, it also includes sands and gravels formed by rivers. The Kazusa Group showing thick deposits is broadly distributed under the southern part of the Kanto Plain, as mentioned in the Close-up column: Tokyo's underground.

Musashino Uplands: originated from the alluvial fans at the bottom of the sea Virtually, Tokyo's landforms are represented by the Musashino Uplands and the lowlands surrounding it: Arakawa, Nakagawa and Tamagawa Lowlands. The northern part of the Musashino Uplands extends towards Saitama Prefecture. In Tokyo proper, its western part extends to the center of Ome City, while its eastern fringes expand from Itabashi Ward (Narimasu), Kita Ward (Akabane), the Ueno Station area to Ota Ward (Den'enchofu area). It shows a triangular shape with the apex in the westmost part of the uplands. Around Ome the elevation is 190 m, while in the east only about 20 m, showing a steep elevational gradient as uplands. This can be explained by the origins of the Musashino Uplands. The main part of the uplands was formed as river terraces originated from alluvial fans of the Tama River. The age of the terraces is from about 130,000 to 10,000 years ago. On the other hand, the eastern part of the uplands was formed as a marine terrace around the peak of the Last Interglacial Stage. We can therefore conclude that the Musashino Uplands consist of terraces of different ages and origins. The origin of these terraces can be traced to long-term crustal movements, sea level oscillations due to climatic changes and oscillations in the amount of precipitation (Ref. 1).

According to the geomorphological map and the classification map of terrace surfaces, it is possible to identify the distribution of the terraces constituting the Musashino Uplands, as there have been a number of such maps issued after the 1950s. Such classifications can be based on topographical maps, aerial photographs or local field surveys. Fig. 1.2 is a compilation of previous classifications. At the same time, use of modern technology like aviation laser survey for the collection of detailed/accurate elevation data, and multiple boring core samples add new insights and help us reconsider the distribution and classification of terraces.

Classification of the Musashino Uplands based on the Kanto Loam
It is difficult to assess the age of the sediments resulted from the action of the rivers and sea. Conversely, the Kanto Loam including volcanic ash and pumice layers, deposited by large-scale volcanic eruptions, can be reliable sources of information about the age of Musashino Uplands landforms, when we know the

age of the volcanic eruption. The keys are the products of eruption such as Hakone Kissawa Lower Tephra Group (about 125,000 years ago), Ontake 1st Tephra (about 100,000 years ago), Hakone Tokyo Tephra (about 70,000 years ago), AT Tephra (about 30,000 years ago), etc. Based on such data, the Musashino Uplands can be divided as follows: terraces older than the Shimosueyoshi Terrace (125,000 years ago), Musashino Terrace Group (100,000 –60,000 years ago), Tachikawa Terrace Group (40,000–10,000 years ago).

Shimosueyoshi Terrace was first identified at Shimosueyoshi, Yokohama City (Kanagawa Prefecture); it was formed 125,000 years ago, at the peak of the Last Interglacial Stage (also known as the Shimosueyoshi period), as a marine terrace. In Tokyo, it is locally known as the Yodobashi and Ebara Uplands, located in Setagaya, Shinjuku, Shibuya, Minato and Shinagawa Wards (Fig. 1.2). Compared with the Musashino Terrace, its specific features include slightly higher elevations and the more developed valleys. The geological composition covering Shimosueyoshi Terrace from the surface is: the Tachikawa–Musashino –Shimosueyoshi Loam Sub-layers representing the Kanto Loam, followed underneath by the sand layers, known as the Tokyo Formation, deposited at the peak of the Last Interglacial Stage (Fig. 1.3) on the bottom of Tokyo Bay (the paleo Tokyo bay), when the coastal line was located approximately in present day Chofu–Mitaka Cities (Fig. 1.4(d)). At the time, the sea level was approximately 5 m higher than the present one, but afterwards due to crustal movements, the sediments including the Tokyo Formation were uplifted to their current

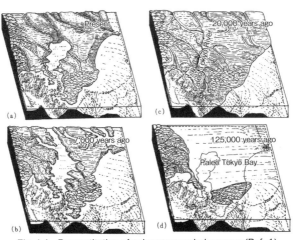

Fig. 1.4 Reconstitution of paleo geomorphology map (Ref. 1)

elevation.

Following the peak of the Last Interglacial Stage, the sea level kept oscillating but the general trend was to gradually lower, until about 20,000 years ago, at the peak of the Last Glacial Maximum, when the sea level was approximatery 120 m lower than the current one.   The coastal line moved towards the sea and on the newly emerged land Tama River flowed freely.   As the river mouth kept getting lower with the lowering sea level, river erosion intensified, and in the lower reaches, the river cut the Shimosueyoshi Terrace formed as the bottom of sea at the peak of the Last Interglacial Stage.   Some areas were left un-eroded, as the Yodobashi and Ebara Uplands.   Between the peak of the Last Interglacial Stage and the peak of the Last Glacial Maximum, there were periods when stable conditions allowed the formation of broad alluvial fans, resulting in the multiple levels of river terraces.   These are classified into two groups, the higher ones known as the Musashino Terrace Group (M_1, M_2, M_3 Terraces in descending order), while the lower ones belong to the Tachikawa Terrace Group (Tc_1, Tc_2, Tc_3 Terraces in descending order).   It is possible to distinguish between these two groups due to the presence of a very clear terrace cliff.   This is named the Kokubunji Cliff Line which extends from northeast of Tachikawa City through the east of Kunitachi Station, Jindaiji, and continues to Futako-tamagawa, with a cliff hight of approximately   10-20 m.   It is the most prominent feature of the Musashino Uplands, and it is marked by a line of natural springs.

Within the Musashino Terrace Group, part of the M_1 Terrace is widespread to the east, locally known as the Narimasu and Toshima Uplands, while the M_2 Terrace is widespread to the northeast, known as the Akabane Uplands.   The Tachikawa Terrace Group is not found in the eastern part of the Musashino Uplands, but is widespread in the western part.   There is large difference in elevation between the Tachikawa Terrace Group and the lowlands along the Tama River, but this difference diminishes towards the east.   The highest of these terraces, Tc_1 Terrace (30,000-40,000 years ago), gradually loses height until reaching Futako-tamagawa, it is difficult to differentiate it from the lowlands and it finally disappears.   Actually, it continues underground for a few kilometers upstream from the river mouth and can be identified at a depth of about 20-30 m below the sea level.   An even newer terrace level, the Tc_3 Terrace, was formed during the coldest period at the peak of the Last Glacial Maximum (approximately 20,000 years ago).   At the time, glaciers expanded in the high latitude areas, and the sea level was approximately 120 m lower than that at present. As a consequence, the Tokyo Bay emerged, and a confluent river of the Ara and Tone Rivers (before being redirected) joined with the Tama River in the area of present-day off Haneda, finally reaching the ocean in the area of present-day Uraga Channel (Fig. 1.4(c)). This river is called the Paleo Tokyo River, and it generated a landform known as the Paleo Tokyo Valley. As a consequence, the areas adjacent to the Paleo Tokyo River and its tributaries are characterized by the presence of depressions which can be continuously traced as deep buried valleys filled with alluvium.

Lowlands and alluvial sediments in Tokyo   After the peak of the Last Glacial Maximum, with general global warming, glaciers in the high latitude areas melted and the sea level gradually rose. As a result, the valley landforms created at the peak of the Last Glacial Maximum were invaded by the sea. The sea level continued to rise and the peak was about 7,000 years ago. At that time, a rias coast forming a indented coast line with inlets along the east margin of the Musashino Uplands had appeared (Fig. 1.4(b)). Especially in the area along the Naka River Lowlands up to the northeastern part of present-day Saitama Prefecture, an inner bay was formed, known as the Inner Tokyo Bay. Its shape was identified since before World War II from the distribution of the shell mounds of the Jomon period. At present, compared with this peak, the current sea level is a few meters lower. Ara, Tone and Tama Rivers continued to provide sediments which created deltas, and reshaped the coastline close to its present configuration. Due to such rapid changes, the valleys formed during the Last Glacial Maximum were filled with sands and muds, and sedimentation continues at present in the outer reaches of the expanding deltas. These sediments are called alluvium, and they continue to be deposited currently at the mouth of rivers in the lowlands along the coast. Due to their young age, these sedimentary geological units are very soft and vulnerable to natural disasters (see Close-up: Tokyo's underground).

The present day Tokyo Bay coastline was further modified/reshaped by the landfills which have continued since the Edo period, taking a geometrical shape. Due to these landfills the coastline advanced at a higher speed than the natural sedimentation rate. As we mentioned above, residential development projects in the Tama Hills kept removing geological formations at a rate far above the natural rate of erosion. It took between a few thousands to 1 million years to create such landforms and geology in Tokyo, but in less than 100 years humans completely transformed it.

(Takehiko Suzuki)

Kanda River and its flow

●**What is Kanda River?** Kanda River is a class A river which originates in the Inokashira pond in Mitaka City (Fig. 1a). It has a total length of 25.5 km and a drainage area of 105 km². Kanda River flows through Suginami, Nakano, Shinjuku, Toshima, Bunkyo, Chiyoda and Taito Wards. It ends when it joins the Sumida River, after the confluence with Zempukuji and Myoshoji Rivers. Among the rivers flowing through the central area of Tokyo Metropolis, it has the widest drainage area (Ref. 1).

The Kanda Josui Waterworks, built in 1629 in the upper reaches of the Kanda River, is the oldest urban water infrastructure in Japan. In the lower reaches, the river was managed as a navigation canal or used as a drainage channel (Ref. 1). The boundary between the upper and lower reaches is Sekiguchi Oaraizeki (Edogawa Park in Bunkyo Ward) where the intake weir was located (Fig. 1e).

During the Edo period, the name of the river differed in the area downstream from Sekiguchi Oaraizeki, with both Edogawa and Kandagawa being used (Ref. 2). This is preserved in some local names such as the above mentioned Edogawa park or Edogawabashi station on the Yurakucho Metro Line. Currently, its entire flow is called the Kanda River, but on some maps, it still appears as Kanda Josui Waterworks.

●**Kanda River's source and its upper reaches** Kanda River's source, the Inokashira Pond, is located in the eastern part of the Musashino Uplands, at an elevation of approximately 50 m and was a natural spring (also see Chapter 4). At present, the natural spring water source is reduced, so that the pond is supplied with pumped groundwater (Fig. 1a). Tokugawa Ieyasu, the first *shogun* of the Edo period, used the pond's water for tea, and ever since it has become famous and the name "water for tea" (Ochanomizu) sticks to it. The link between its name and that of the Ochanomizu Station, located along the river's lower reaches, is very interesting.

In the area where the river crosses the Keio Inokashira Line, close to the Inokashirakoen Station, the Kanda River is still a stream, but its course soon gets cast in concrete on 3 sides. It is followed by a parallel walking path, popular with local joggers, and surrounded by green areas and parks, with carps and water fowl, making the place a very pleasant landscape.

●**Intake of water from the Tamagawa Josui Waterworks and water management policies** At the intersection with the ring road no. 8 (Kampachi), in the proximity of the Takaido Station on the Inokashira Line, the water flow of the Kanda River increases (Fig. 1b). This is thanks to a plan to revive the flow of fresh water in Tokyo, which linked Tamagawa Josui Waterworks and the Kanda River. At Tamagawa Upper Stream Water Management Center, the water is purified at an advanced degree, and sent back to the Kanda River, enriching its volume. Since the 1960s, the purification has improved water quality and allowed the recovery of habitat for fish and other aquatic life.

Continuing east, the Kanda River crosses the ring road no. 7 (Kannana), where an important facility is located; it is the underground retention pond (Fig. 1c). As a consequence of urbanization in the Kanda River drainage area, rain water could not be absorbed by the land surface during heavy rain and typhoons. There were some episodes of flooding occurrences especially in the 1970–1990s, so that setting up such facilities became a priority.

Currently, the Kanda River drainage area can safely withstand rain up to 50 mm/hour, thanks to the combination of such water retention facilities as anti-flood ponds and flood-control channels (Ref. 1, 2). The underground retention pond at the intersection with the ring road no. 7, which is built as a tunnel under the road, has the capacity to retain 540,000 m³ of water in the eventuality of severe rainstorm (Ref. 3) (Fig. 1c). Furthermore, close to the city center, there are 4 more flood control channels (Fig. 1d). These re-direct the water flow when river water level increases and prevent flooding, solving the problem of flooding along the Kanda River.

●From Kanda Josui Waterworks to Sumida River   During the Edo period, the Kanda Josui Waterworks had its intake weir at Sekiguchi Oaraizeki (Fig. 1e), and after passing the Mito domain's city residence (at present, Koishikawa Korakuen Garden), the water was transported using wooden pipes which over-crossed Edo Castle's outer moat, to Kanda, Nihonbashi and Kyobashi neighborhoods. Vestiges of such wooden pipes were discovered between JR (Japan Railways) Suidobashi and Ochanomizu Stations (Fig. 1f). This is actually the origin of the name of Suidobashi.

At last, Kanda River meets Sumida River at the Yanagibashi bridge in Taito Ward. This is a densely built area and the visibility is reduced, but the view of the Tokyo Skytree from the Sumida River terrace is quite remarkable. We do not show a photo of it so that the readers should feel compelled to go there and take a look by themselves.

(Hiroshi Matsuyama)

Fig. 1   Landscape along Kanda River
(a) Springing point at Inokashira Pond, (b) Confluence of Tamagawa Josui Waterworks and the Kanda River at Takaido, (c) Entry of the underground retention pond at the ring road no. 7, along with the intake facility of the Kanda River, (d) Takadanobaba floodway, (e) Guide plate of intake weir of Kanda Josui Waterworks at Edogawa Park, and (f) Monument of wooden pipes of Kanda Josui Waterworks near JR Suidobashi station.   (All photos by Hiroshi Matsuyama in March 2019)

Tokyo's underground

●**The ignored underground** When traveling in Tokyo, in many instances you have to travel underground: the subway obviously so, even the Tokyo highway system sometimes goes underground. However, we don't pay much attention to the underground space just outside of the tunnels. We are more familiar with the higher places, such as the Tokyo Skytree and its 634 m height, or the height of Mt. Fuji, 3,776 m. The underground is usually ignored, very few people aware of what lays 10 m, 100 m or 100 km underneath their houses.

On the other hand, there are many issues related to our daily lives, such as the falsification of data regarding the pillars which support high-rise apartments, the liquefaction occurring during major earthquakes or the land subsidence due to excessive groundwater exploitation, so people should be more aware of the underground. This is especially important in Tokyo, where space is at a premium and we rely on underground space to a large extent.

●**Soft sediments of the underground in the lowlands: the alluvium** The most challenging problems are caused by the soft underground sediments. The alluvium deposited by the rivers or the sea becomes compact with the passage of time. However, after less than 10,000 years, the deposits are still soft. Such young deposits accumulated during the past 10,000 years including the present are called alluvium, and are to be found in the underground in lowlands of Tokyo, so-called Tokyo downtown, mainly represented by soft sand and mud deposits.

The distribution of these layers can be estimated from the landforms. In the eastern and southern areas of the 23 wards where the elevation is lower than a few meters above sea level, the underground layers mostly consist of alluvium. Even at higher elevations, alluvium can be found along the rivers. So, it is possible to understand the distribution of alluvium from the landforms, but their thickness can only be known based on core drilling surveys. In Tokyo there is an

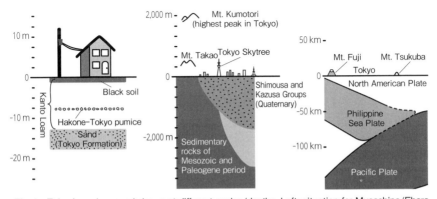

Fig. 1 Tokyo's underground shown at different scales/depths. Left: situation for Musashino/Ebara and Yodobashi Uplands. Center and right: by author based of Ref.1 (modified).

amazing number of drilling survey sites. According to results of surveys, while the upper ground surface of these layers can be flat, the bottom surface is irregular, and in some places these layers can be over 50 m thick.

●**Underground sediments as witnesses of paleo landforms**   Sediments older than the alluvium can be found underneath, or in the Musashino Uplands where these can be found below 1 m in depth. The most superficial sediments of the Musashino Uplands is the Kanto Loam, consisting of volcanic ashes, pumice and soils, all carried by the wind and deposited here.   In the uplands area, the thickest loam layers are approximately 15 m.   Under these, there are the layers of sands and gravels carried by rivers or the sands and muds deposited at the bottom of sea, all consistent with the uplands landforms. These are called terrace deposits and their typical thickness is under 20 m, in close relation with the landforms (Fig. 1).

Furthermore, directly under the terrace deposits there is a succession of sands, gravels and muds.   From the top, these are called the Shimousa and Kazusa Groups, and they are the equivalent of similar sediments found in the Boso Peninsula (Chiba Prefecture).   In some instances, the sediments of the Shimousa Group might be missing. These layers belong to the Quaternary, a recent geological era, and were deposited over the past 2.6 million years.   Analyzing these layers' depth, age and composition might serve as a clue to understanding of paleo landforms in Tokyo.   During the early Quaternary, the area of present-day central Tokyo was under the sea (more than 500 m deep), which was subsequently uplifted and emerged as land.   Due to climate changes, the sea level has oscillated.   These changes can be "read" from the Kazusa Group.   The bottom of these sediments can be found at more than 1,000 m depth under central Tokyo, but it is found shallower in the Tama area—a few hundred meters around Akishima City, and are a continuation of harder formations found in the Kanto Mountains, formed during the Mesozoic and the Paleogene.

●**Stack of plates in the deeper underground**   Next, we are going to explore even deeper, at depths of more than 10 km, an area difficult to reach by core drilling. Tokyo is located above the North American Plate.   However, at depths of around 20–30 km, there is the boundary with the Philippine Sea Plate, and deeper, at about 80–90 km depth there is the boundary with the Pacific Plate, respectively.   It is very rare that some overlapping major plates can be found under a big city.   It is well known that strong earthquakes occur along plate boundaries, so this is why the history of Tokyo is closely linked with earthquake disasters.

From the above, we understand that the underground of Tokyo is very complex, and there are different stories to be told about the geology depending on depths.   Comparing with other large metropolises like London or New York, the latter have far simpler undergrounds, and except for the superficial sediments, they are composed of harder rocks, showing strong and stable foundations.   By comparison, the underground structure in Tokyo is complicated and unstable.   This is caused by Tokyo's location in an area influenced by dynamic and active crustal movement.   (Takehiko Suzuki)

Earthquakes and countermeasures

●Tokyo: A history of natural disasters

It is difficult to separate Tokyo from its history of disasters caused by earthquakes. This goes as far back as the beginnings of the city around A.D.1600. At the geological time scale, this period of approximately 400 years is a brief moment. However, during this brief time span, three large-scale earthquakes occurred: in 1703 the Genroku Kanto Earthquake, in 1855 the Ansei Edo Earthquake, followed in 1923 by the Taisho Kanto Earthquake. At the same time, Tokyo was also plagued by various other natural disasters, such as flooding and volcanic ash fall, as well as massive scale fires and war-caused destruction.

For Tokyo, it has been a cycle of repeated disasters followed by reconstruction. In the 70 years after the end of World War II, with no earthquake causing major natural disaster, the city continued to expand. But the probability of another big earthquake in Tokyo is very high.

●Disaster caused by earthquakes in Tokyo

In the following paragraphs, we explain about the earthquakes affecting Tokyo, the probability of such an earthquake in the near future and potential measures to deal with it. Three plates and two plate boundaries underlie Tokyo (see close-up: Tokyo's underground, Fig. 1). Along the plate boundaries, large scale subduction zone earthquakes of magnitude (M) 8 class occur. Examples of such subduction-zone earthquakes occurring at the contact of the North American Plate with the Philippine Sea Plate are the Genroku Kanto and Taisho Kanto Earthquakes.

Earthquakes can occur even within the plate. In the shallowest North American Plate, multiple active faults such as the Tachikawa Fault in Tokyo and the Ayasegawa Fault in Saitama are present. Their activity has the potential to cause inland earthquakes up to class M 7. Compared with subduction-zone earthquakes, they are less destructive but since they are shallow, it is estimated that their potential consequences for limited areas can be quite destructive due to strong seismic motion.

Even in the deeper Philippine Sea Plate, earthquakes can occur. There are still many unsolved questions on the Edo Ansei Earthquake, but it is assumed that it occurred under the north part of the Tokyo Bay, within the Philippine Sea Plate.

The epicenters of earthquakes causing disaster in the Tokyo area are known to some extent, and long-term forecasting of the next one has been examined. For instance, it is assumed that an earthquake of the same type as the Genroku Kanto and Taisho Kanto Earthquakes won't occur soon. The reason is that it is believed that the first one has a cycle of occurrence of 2,000–3,000 years, while the later 200–400 years.

●Earthquakes occurring below the Tokyo Capital Region

Conversely, it is feared that a M 7 earthquake can occur directly below the Tokyo capital region. The seismic activity in the period between the Genroku Kanto Earthquake and the Taisho Kanto Earthquake has been comparatively slow in the 70–80 years following the first, but afterwards, a series of M 7 earthquakes preceded the later. 90 years have passed since the Taisho Kanto Earthquake and it is supposed that the period of calm is coming to an end.

Therefore, it is predicted that a few M7 earthquakes will occur before the next M8 earthquake, estimating its probability at 70% over the next 30 years (Ref. 1).

●**Preparing for earthquakes** Despite this kind of long-term predictions regarding the occurrence of earthquakes, it is actually very difficult to predict the exact timing over the short term. On the other hand, in order to reduce the impacts, preparations are possible at the level of people, families, areas and administrative units. One such measure is to be aware of earthquake vulnerability for each area. Currently, each administrative unit announces the earthquake vulnerability. Tokyo Metropolitan Government conducts an earthquake vulnerability assessment every 5 years (Ref. 2). Its results are represented in a map that ranks the risk for each area (Fig. 1). Such measurements are taken at 5,177 spots and for each the risk is graded on a scale of 5. According to the most recent measurements, 85 areas in Tokyo have a risk of 5.

Fig. 1 shows the building collapse risk, the fire risk and the emergency response difficulty. The map for building collapse risk takes into account the topographical and geological conditions and the number of buildings by building type. The former includes: for the lowlands the risk of vibrations and liquefaction, for the hills the impact of extensive land reclamation fills. On the map, landforms are well reflected, for example in eastern Tokyo and the lower reaches of the Tama River the risk is higher. In the area along the ring road no. 7, the particularities of the buildings are also reflected in the higher risk.

Regarding the fire risk, it is higher in the areas with high density of wooden buildings with low resistance to fire and where there are no fire blocking belts. The combined risk map synthesizing all the data above shows the similar pattern of fire risk maps. The first step in order to be able to reduce the impacts is for each citizen to be aware of this map and to understand the risk for the area where they live.   (Takehiko Suzuki)

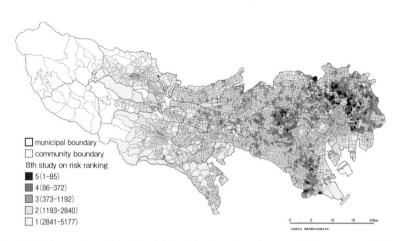

municipal boundary
community boundary
8th study on risk ranking
■ 5(1–85)
■ 4(86–372)
■ 3(373–1192)
□ 2(1193–2840)
□ 1(2841–5177)

0   5   10   15   20km

Fig. 1   Most recent map of combined risk ranking by earthquake vulnerability assesment (Ref. 2)

Mt. Fuji and Tokyo

●**Tokyo and volcanoes** Compared with other metropolises in the world, landforms and geology of Tokyo have been formed under the influence of extremely active geological processes, as we have already explained earlier in this chapter. The influence of volcanic activity is also very strong. It is important to note that of all Japan's 47 prefectures Tokyo has the largest number of active volcanoes. Of the total 111 active volcanoes in Japan, more than 10%, that is 14 active volcanoes (21 if we include the submarine ones), are found in Tokyo. They all belong to the Izu and Ogasawara Islands. Because Tokyo's 23 wards and the area of Tama are located on the east side of the volcanic front which crosses the whole Japanese Archipelago, there are no volcanoes in this area. From Shinjuku, where the Metropolitan government is located, to the closest active volcanoes, Mt. Hakone and Mt. Fuji, the distance is about 80–95 km. This means that there are no fatal risks such as ballistic projectiles of volcanic rocks, pyroclastic flows and volcanic sector collapse in Tokyo. However, in case of eruption, there is a risk of ash fall and volcanic mudflows (lahar) even in more distant areas from the volcanoes. Even in Tokyo's 23 wards and in the Tama area there are predictions of ash fall in case of volcanic activity (Ref. 1). Such ash fall is especially possible in case of the eruption of Mt. Fuji.

●**Mt. Fuji and Tokyo's location** Mt. Fuji is visible from Tokyo's 23 wards and from the Tama area (Fig. 1). It is somehow hidden behind some other mountain ranges, so that its lower slopes are not visible, but the upper half is visible. Actually one of the attractions of living in Tokyo is enjoying the beautiful view of this volcanic landform. This visibility also means that volcanic erup-

Fig. 1 View of Mt. Fuji from the sky above Haneda Airport
In the foreground, Tonezawa Mts., Southwest Kanto Plain and the lower reaches of Tama River (photo by Takehiko Suzuki in March 2003).

tion of Mt. Fuji is most likely to influence Tokyo, and Tokyo's location east of Mt. Fuji has a very important significance.

Checking past records, we are able to understand the extent of the impact of Mt. Fuji's eruptions on Tokyo. There are actually 2 types of such records: the written records of past people, but also to the records kept in the geological layers. We shall look into these records to better understand the relation between Mt. Fuji and Tokyo.

●**The Hōei Volcanic Eruption during the Edo period**   The most recent eruption of Mt. Fuji is the Hōei Eruption, which occurred in the middle of the Edo period, in December 1707. During this eruption, a high eruption column (over 10 km high) was emitted from the Hōei crater located on the slope of the Mt. Fuji. This has been an explosive eruption, with the resulting volcanic materials carried by the prevailing westerly winds towards Edo (Tokyo), where historical records show they were deposited in layers more than a few centimeters thick.

The main features of this eruption are that it is the largest in scale during the history of the past 100,000 years of Mt. Fuji's activity and that as a result of a rare Dacite type magma (with a comparatively high SiO_2 content), whitish pumice was deposited, followed by a typical Mt. Fuji's characteristic basaltic black scoria (with a similar configuration with pumice). This was recorded in Edo by Arai Hakuseki in his *Oritaku Shiba no Ki* as follows: "on the 23rd, following the earthquake on the night before, since around noon there was a sound like thunder and then white ash similar to snow started to fall .... Beginning on the 25th, black ash started

to fall ...." The Hōei Eruption had an important impact on most areas around Mt. Fuji, from the eastern half of Shizuoka to the western half of Kanagawa Prefectures. However, its impact on Edo was relatively limited. If such an eruption were to occur nowadays, in our technological society with its complicated infrastructure, the impact would decidedly be deeper.

●**The geological record of the eruptions**
Among previous large scale volcanic eruptions of Mt. Fuji, Jōgan Eruption occurred during the Heian period. During this eruption large quantities of lava flowed, but it is thought that the ash fall did not affect Tokyo. However, there are no historical records of this eruption, but there are geological layers to prove the ash fall. This is the Kanto Loam, which covers large areas of Tokyo's uplands and hills that originated from ashes and soils from the volcanic eruptions. The Kanto Loam deposited over the past 100,000 years mainly originated in the ashes of the many eruptions of Mt. Fuji. Following each explosive eruption like the Hōei Eruption, the volcanic ash would be carried by the winds and deposited, resulting in the formation of the Kanto Loam. The winds carrying the volcanic ash are the prevailing westerly winds and in most situations the ash is carried eastward. While in Tokyo's area on average approximately 1 m of Kanto Loam was deposited over 10,000 years, in Shizuoka, on the west side of Mt. Fuji, the equivalent layers are missing. Therefore, from the point of view of ash fall, there is a close relationship between Mt. Fuji and Tokyo.

(Takehiko Suzuki)

Chapter 2 **Tokyo's Climate**

Surface meteorological observatory "Tokyo" of the Japan Meteorological Agency (JMA) that moved to Kitanomaru Park from Otemachi (photo by Hideo Takahashi in September 2016)

In this chapter on Tokyo's climate (including the islands), we shall first analyze the seasonal changes, their specific features and their backdrop. Next, based on various sources of observational data, we shall focus on the seasonal distribution of precipitation, temperatures, winds and their inter-relations, and their combined impact on the urban climate.

2.1 Geographical factors which influence Tokyo's climate

Tokyo is situated on the eastern coast of the Japanese Archipelago facing the Pacific Ocean, which marks the eastern border of the Asian Continent, at temperate latitudes, so seasonal changes are very clear: during winter it is under the influence of northwesterly cold winds from the continent, while during summer it is under the influence of southerly winds from the Pacific Ocean which bring hot temperatures and much humidity. The Kanto Plain, where Tokyo is located, is bordered towards the north by the Mikuni and Echigo Mountains and towards the west by the Kanto Mountains respectively with high elevation, so during winter sunny and dry weather conditions are frequent. On the other hand, to the east and south it faces the ocean; furthermore, Tokyo Bay penetrates deeply from the south. The distribution of land and ocean, and the configuration of major landforms are the sources of local winds such as the land and sea breezes or the mountain and valley breezes. At regional scale, the atmospheric phenomena which are themselves a characteristic of regional climate, and the expanding urbanization generating the heat island (a huge problem in Tokyo), show complex interactions.

2.2　Seasonal variation in Tokyo's precipitation and temperature

Fig. 2.1 illustrates the average precipitation and temperature seasonal changes in central Tokyo (Chiyoda Ward). The data cover an interval of 30 years (1981–2010) and are based on the pentad value, the average of every 5 day starting on January 1st, showing the average temperature and the accumulated sum of precipitations resulting in 73 pentad values; this offers a higher resolution view of seasonal changes than the monthly averages.

Seasonal change of precipitation　Tokyo's average precipitation is 1528.8 mm per year, so the pentad average is 20.9 mm. Quantities higher than this average are frequent from mid-March to mid-October. However, the seasonal variation of precipitation is more complex than the temperature variation, with multiple maximum periods. *Baiu* (or *Tsuyu*), the early summer rainy season from mid-June to mid-July, and *Akisame*, the autumn rain and typhoon season centered on late September, are separated by a period of minimum precipitation during the interval when the Pacific High prevails over Japan. In Tokyo and generally in eastern Japan, there is a trend that the autumn/typhoon rainy season brings more precipitation than the early summer rainy season. Other periods with higher precipitation are the *Natane-zuyu*, a minor rainy interval at the end of March to the beginning of April; the *Hashiri-zuyu* in mid-May and the *Sazanka-zuyu* in the second half of November.

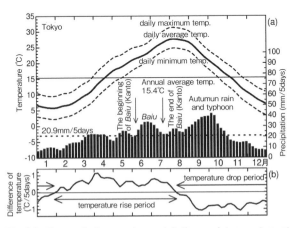

Fig. 2.1　Seasonal changes in precipitation and temperature at Tokyo based on pentad values (1981-2010)

Seasonal change of temperature   The seasonal variation in temperature is simpler than that of precipitation, a salient feature being the slower pace of temperature increase in June. This temporary stagnation coincides with the first half of the *Baiu* season, before the increase in precipitation, and is followed by a rapid increase in temperature in the second half of the *Baiu* season in July. This occurs because the cloudy and rainy weather reduces the quantity of solar radiation, but also because of the activity of the Okhotsk High which brings a flow of cold air to the Tohoku area and influences the Kanto area as the "cold *Baiu* interval". On the other hand, during the second half of the *Baiu* season, the influence of the Pacific High becomes stronger, with southern winds bringing in hot and humid air masses. Rainfall type is also different, with drizzle being characteristic for the first half of the *Baiu* season, while occasional torrential rains follow during the second half. As for the temperature increase, it is most notable at the beginning of April, during the *Natane-zuyu*, when it gets warmer after each rain.

The difference between the central city and the island area   Next, we compare the seasonal climatic variation between the central area of Tokyo and the islands. Figs. 2.2 and 2.3 show seasonal variation of the precipitation and temperature for Hachijojima in the southern Izu Islands and the Chichijima in the Ogasawara Islands. The average annual precipitation amount in Hachijojima is 3202.4 mm (43.9 mm per pentad), the highest value for Tokyo Metropolis. Meanwhile, Chichijima records 1292.5 mm (17.8 mm per pentad), less than central Tokyo. The increase in precipitation during the *Baiu* season is very clear for all 3 locations, with the gradual advance of the *Baiu* front towards the north manifested in the arrival of the rainy season in Tokyo 1 month later than in

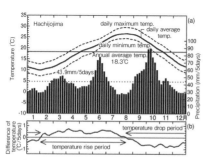

Fig. 2.2   Same as Fig. 2.1 but for Hachijojima

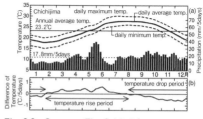

Fig. 2.3   Same as Fig. 2.1 but for Chichijima

Chichijima.   The season of low precipitation following the *Baiu* season in Chichijima coincides with the peak of the rainy *Baiu* season in Tokyo.   On the other hand, there is a very clear difference between Tokyo and Hachijojima in terms of the arrival of the autumn rainy season and typhoon season as response to the southern shift of the autumn rainy front.   Meanwhile, in Chichijima a slight increase in precipitation occurs between September and November, but it does not show a seasonal concentration.   In a similar manner, at the end of winter and beginning of spring, snow occurs in Tokyo proper (see Close-up: Snow in Tokyo) due to the migration of the extra-tropical cyclone along the southern coast of Japan, and an increase in precipitation both in Hachijojima and Tokyo proper can be observed, but there is no such increase in Chichijima. Ogasawara Islands show a different pattern of precipitation from the rest of the Tokyo Metropolis.   Concerning the seasonal changes of temperature, in Chichijima the daily average temperatures are even during winter around 17℃, while in summer they are 28℃, with a smaller annual range of average temperature, and the maximum and minimum occuring approximately half month later than in Tokyo; the same trends can be identified in Hachijojima.

Difference between central Tokyo and the western inland sector   In order to compare the climate of central Tokyo and the western sector, we use Fig. 2.4a, which shows differences in average precipitation in central Tokyo and Hachioji City.   The average precipitation in Hachioji is 1602.3 mm, slightly higher than in central Tokyo, mainly during mid-summer.   During summer, thunderstorms frequently occur in the mountainous region including the Kanto Mountains range due to solar heating and orographic effects, so that the precipitation amount declines from the west towards the east of the southern Kanto area.   During all other seasons, precipitation is under the strong influence

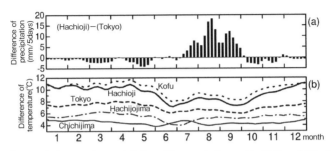

Fig. 2.4   (a) Seasonal changes in precipitation difference between Hachioji and Tokyo, (b) daily temperature range at various stations based on pentad value climatology (1981-2010)

of the frontal activity and migration of the extra-tropical cyclone along the southern coast of Japan, so that while precipitation increases from the northern area of Tokyo towards the south, no such difference occurs between the western and eastern parts of the Metropolitan area.

Fig. 2.4b shows the seasonal changes in multi-yearly average of diurnal temperature range, based on daily maximum and minimum temperatures. The daily temperature amplitudes are more pronounced during the cold season than the warm season, with an amplitude of approximately 7℃ in Tokyo and approximately 10℃ in Hachioji during the cold season. In Hachioji, approximately 40 km inland west from central Tokyo, the daily temperature amplitudes are similar with Kofu, a typical inland basin in Yamanashi Prefecture. While the daily maximum temperatures are not very different between Tokyo and Hachioji, during winter the daily minimum temperatures are on average 4℃ lower in Hachioji, and daily temperature amplitude is higher in Hachioji. Comparatively, the islands, surrounded by the ocean, show lower daily temperature amplitudes, averaging 4-5℃ all year round.

2.3　Distribution of temperatures in Tokyo

Urban climate is the result of natural climate modified under the influence of urbanization, and a representative example is the urban heat island. This phenomenon, not limited to Tokyo, clearly appears during winter, manifesting as a combination of clear weather and weak wind conditions between nightfall and early morning. In the following section, we focus on the temperature distribution during typical conditions of the heat island formation during winter in early morning, and the daytime temperatures during summer, which cause heatstroke and increased consumption of electricity.

Temperature distribution during winter nights　　Fig. 2.5 shows the distribution of average temperatures at 6 o'clock on winter mornings with clear weather and weak wind conditions for 37 cases. Besides data from the JMA's AMeDAS (Automated Meteorological Data Acquisition System), data of air pollution monitoring stations provided by local governments, as well as by a network of university and research bodies (E-METROS), overall data for 124 locations were used. According to such detailed data, the highest temperature was recorded in Chuo Ward (Ginza neighborhood), and it decreases steeply towards the west and east, as shown by the narrow distance between the

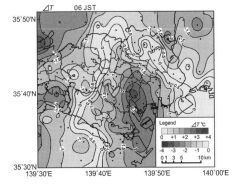

Fig. 2.5 Average temperature distribution in the Tokyo-wards area and its surroundings under clear-sky and weak-wind conditions at 06:00 JST (Ref. 1)

Temperature distribution is shown as a temperature deviation from spatial average temperature. Contour lines are drawn at every 0.5℃.

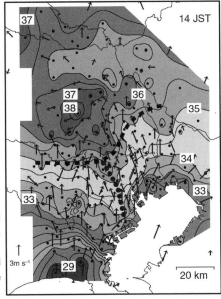

Fig. 2.6 Temperature and surface wind distribution recorded on 4 August 2006. (Ref. 2)

The sea breeze front is shown by the dashed line. The convergence line is shown by the dotted line.

isotherms.   While the location of highest temperature and the steep difference does not change much during the night, temperature difference of 3–4℃ in the wards area of Tokyo becomes clear gradually.

Distribution of daytime temperatures during summer   Distribution of daytime temperatures in Tokyo during summer is under the strong influence of the sea breeze.   We shall explain in more detail the shift between the sea breeze and the land breeze later, but here we mention that compared with the sea, which has insignificant temperature differences between day and night, the land shows differences between higher temperatures during daytime and lower temperatures at night. The breeze therefore blows from the cooler sea towards the land during daytime, and during nighttime from the land towards the sea; in the case of Tokyo, the daytime sea breeze blows from the south, while during night, the breeze blows from the north or the west towards the sea. When the sea breeze from the south, from the area of Tokyo Bay and Sagami Bay blows through the city in the afternoon, temperature maximum in the southern area of Saitama prefecture appears as shown in Fig. 2.6, with higher temperature in the northern areas of the metropolis. The cool wind originates over the sea, so that the coastal areas are cooler, but as the breeze warms over the land, it affects areas further away inland. The forefront of the invading sea breeze is called a sea breeze front, and it reaches the southern part of Saitama Prefecture around noon. As the wind in the vicinity of the sea breeze front is weak, the stagnant air has time to heat over the land so it loses its original cooling effect.

Another characteristic feature of temperature distribution in and around Tokyo is the wedge shape of the area of higher temperatures, extending from southern Saitama to the southern area of the metropolis. The cause is not clear yet, but it is thought to originate in the fact that while the sea breeze from the Sagami Bay is a southerly wind, the one from the Tokyo Bay is slightly easterly, so that the two winds converge in the western area of the metropolis. In this area of convergence, the wind speed slows down, so it can be assumed that it results in the heating of stagnant air from the land surface.

 ## 2.4 Sea breeze/land breeze alternation

The formation of sea breeze and land breeze (similar to mountain breeze/valley breeze), depends to a large extent on the distribution of sea and land masses, the landforms. The direction of respective winds does not change much, however, when the wind speed is low around the time of the shift of direction, there might be variation of direction. We analyzed the timing of the shifts in wind during summer clear days in the metropolis, which resulted in Fig. 2.7.

According to Fig. 2.7a, during daytime, the sea breeze starts around 9 o'clock in the morning in the coastal area of Tokyo Bay and Sagami Bay, it reaches the central area of Tokyo around 11 o'clock and the southern areas of Saitama Prefecture around noon. Meanwhile, isochrones east of the Kanto Mountains show the gradual expansion of the area where the easterly valley breeze forms to blow towards the mountains. Simultaneously, there is a similar process occurring with the southerly valley breeze blowing towards the north. In the southern sector of Saitama Prefecture there is an area where the shift is late, due to the intersection of the sea breeze and valley breeze, but after 2 p.m. these two merge and the southerly wind from the Kanto plain expands, producing the so-called "extended sea breeze".

At night however, the land breeze formed in the southern area of Saitama Prefecture and central Tokyo, where the southerly wind blows all night, is not usually affected by the sea breeze. Fig. 2.7b shows the time of the change of wind in the situation when the land breeze reaches the coast of Tokyo Bay; as the land breeze is very slow compared with the sea breeze, it takes time, so it reaches the coast around 5 o'clock.

The reason of this delay or of the fact that the inland breeze rarely reaches central Tokyo is that at night, central Tokyo is warm due to an area of convergence of low pressure air which blocks the inland breeze front (Ref. 4). In addition, the rough urban surface (due to concentration of buildings) slows down the wind speed, so that the land breeze cannot penetrate, thus influencing the local wind patterns. Furthermore, it is thought that during summer nights, in the area of the Tokyo Bay, relatively strong south-western winds occur towards the Boso Peninsula (Ref. 5), which do not allow the land breeze to blow towards the south. (Hideo Takahashi)

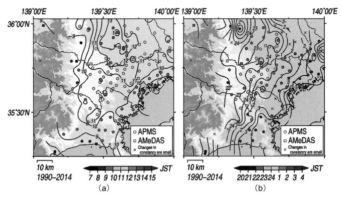

Fig. 2.7 Distribution map showing the wind system transition time during (a) the daytime and (b) the nighttime (Ref. 3)
As for (b), cases when land breeze arrives to the coastal area of Tokyo were used for analysis.

Why summer in Tokyo is not only "hot" but also "humid"?

●**Hot and humid summer** Why are summers in Tokyo and in the Kanto area so hot and humid? Might it be the influence of the much-debated climate change? Or is it because Tokyo is such a big metropolis? Or are there other factors involved?

●**Hot summer following the *Baiu* rainy season** Although the large-scale atmospheric flows do not change significantly before and after the *Baiu* rainy season, there are many wet and chilly days during the rainy season. However, when the Western Pacific Subtropical High covers Japan, the temperature rises dramatically, marking the beginning of the "hot summer". Under the Western Pacific Subtropical High, there is a very slow descending air motion, which suppresses clouds. During such clear weather conditions, the land surface is heated by the strong solar radiation. Recently, in addition to the Western Pacific Subtropical High (Fig. 1) the impact of the Tibetan High (located in the upper troposphere) on hot summers in Japan has been also discussed. Here, the Western Pacific Subtropical High and Tibetan High are associated with the rainfall activity of the South and Southeast Asian monsoon. Therefore, to understand summer in Japan, it is necessary to study the climate of the broader tropical monsoon regions. In any case, the effect of solar radiation is very significant. In fact, the downward air flow under a subtropical high is also important. Why should we focus on the impact of downward air flow on hot weather? As an analogy, when riding on an airplane, atmospheric air temperature falls with altitude, so the air temperature is lower in the upper atmosphere. However, under the same at-

mospheric pressure conditions, the air masses in the high atmosphere should be warmer, as we shall explain.

●**Temperature increase and humidity decline due to the descending air motion** If we could experimentally bring an air mass from the upper atmosphere adiabatically down to the sea level (pressure must be the same as the sea level atmosphere), it would be possible to confirm that the air mass of the upper atmosphere is warmer. In reality, this experiment is impossible, so this is only a hypothetical example. In the upper atmosphere, airplanes cool the air in the plane at higher pressure. If the cooling system breaks down, passengers might get heat stroke. Actually, when it is cold in the airplane, this is not because of the low temperatures outside, but due to the cooling system. In the upper atmosphere, there is no water vapor supply source, so the air is very dry. Again, if we bring an air mass in the upper atmosphere at the same pressure as the one at sea level, it should be warm, but at the lower pressures in the upper atmosphere the temperature is low. Here the equation of saturated water vapor as a function of temperature can be useful. According to it, with the increase in air temperature, the capacity for water vapor retention also increases. As a consequence, cool air masses in the upper atmosphere are very dry.

●**Might it be the influence of urbanization?** We might also be concerned by the influence of urbanization. Generally speaking, with the spread of urbanization, the air tends to become drier. This is because the human-made surfaces expand, at the cost of natural soil and vegetation areas. Compared with concrete and asphalt surfaces, natural soil and vegetation retain more humidity, so that at the same amount of solar radiation, more of it is used as energy for evaporation, and less energy is used for heating the lower atmosphere. This is why among the direct consequences of urbanization are a rise in temperatures and drought. Based on long-term observations, we can state that Tokyo is increasingly drier, so urbanization plays no role in the "hot and humid" summer weather.

●**A reason for "humid" summers**   As explained above, the reason for the summer heat in the Kanto area is the Pacific High, but for the humidity we need to look for additional causes. We need to find the source of water vapor. One of these possible sources is the Kuroshio ocean current, flowing south of Japan, and the warm sea surface. The higher temperatures of the sea surface mean increased quantities of vapor supply into the atmosphere. Higher quantities of

water vapor add to the effects the landforms have on thermodynamics, so it is assumed that the water vapor is transported to the coast of Kanto by the summer monsoon flows.   Our previous research shows that during extremely humid and hot summers, the sea surface temperature south of Kanto is higher, generating more vapor and thus determining the hotter and more humid summers in Tokyo (Ref. 1).   We can therefore state that on the backdrop of global warming, compared with other regions, Tokyo is hotter and more humid.   Moreover, the recent long term warming of the sea surface in areas of the Kuroshio is much higher than the average of the global ocean. Tokyo is therefore getting hotter and more humid due to the impact of multiple causes, among which the impact of the distant El Niño (the Southern Oscillation) or the complex interactions between the atmosphere, the land and the sea.   This explains why forecasting summer weather is so difficult.

(Hiroshi Takahashi)

Fig. 1   Schematic diagram of "the hot and humid Japanese summer mechanism"

Snow in Tokyo

●**Snow causing chaos in Tokyo** From a social perspective, snow in Tokyo causes many problems. These seem minor from the perspective of someone used to snow, but they represent a great hurdle for other areas. In Tokyo and generally in the Kanto region, winter and snow cause both joy and worry. For those young at heart, snow represents joy, but from a social perspective, the impact on traffic and on citizens' daily life is quite a big problem.

●**It is difficult to forecast snow in Tokyo** From the point of view of weather forecast, Tokyo's snow is difficult to predict. The probability of an accurate forecast is around 50%. It is well known that snow in Tokyo is brought by the extra-tropical cyclone along Japan's southern coast. With such a name it sounds as something special, but it is actually a very regular warm, low pressure air system of the lower to mid-latitudes, located around the southern coast of Japan and advancing in a east-north-east direction. Usually, the probability of accurately forecasting the activity of such warm, low pressure air systems is quite high. However, among these low pressure systems, the tropical low pressure systems such as typhoons are difficult to forecast. The same goes for the dynamic of the *Baiu* front during the rainy season.

Among the reasons that make forecasting of snow in Tokyo difficult, we could name the difficulty in predicting the air temperature above land, which is the main determinant of snow vs. rain. It is also related to Tokyo's geographical conditions: Tokyo's winter average temperature is actually very close to the temperature border between snow and rain.

It also reflects the scale and accuracy of the data used in forecasts, for instance details of the land surface etc. For example, under snow cover conditions, more solar radiation is reflected, so the land surface receives less heat. Less heat and lower temperatures above land result in less clouds.

With the snow cover lasting longer, the higher reflection coefficient (called albedo) lasts longer. The influence of this repeated causal chain of snow-albedo-air temperature change is called "ice albedo feedback" and its variations might have an impact on our capacity to forecast the weather. This is a research area which needs improvement. On the other hand, the "ice albedo feedback" is also an important element linked with global warming, and it is researched from various perspectives.

●**The influence of Kuroshio's meander on snow in Tokyo** In April 2019 a major issue was Kuroshio ocean cuurent's large meander which started in 2018. It is assumed that during Kuroshio's large meander, there is a trend for snow to fall in Tokyo; but is it true? The author's recent research demonstrates that the changes in sea surface temperature in the area south of Kanto due to Kuroshio's large meander do not seem to have an influence on snowfall. The issue is not yet elucidated, for instance, how does Kuroshio's meander change the direction of low air pressure masses is yet to be solved. It is assumed that the change of direction of low air pressure masses has a direct influence on the formation of snow vs. rain.

●**Are heavy snowfall events occurring more often recently?** Focusing only on recent events, we are going to consider if heavy snowfall events are really increasing. We use weather data in order to assess this statement: data of the total depth of snow cover (the sum of snow accumulated every day) during the 3 months from December to February (see Fig. 1). Japan Meteorological Agency provides such data since 1961, which means a series of data covering approximately 60 years. According to Fig.1, compared with the 2000s, it seems that recently there is slightly more snow, but in the past there have been other periods with more snow (such as the late 1970s, or the early 1990s), so that we can say that there is no such trend for more snowfall. One concern remains though, the fact that the data series covers such a short time span. For earlier times there are written data, so we should corroborate data for the past 100 years to be able to accurately understand the changes in climate and in snowfall in Tokyo.

●**Vague definition of heavy snow**　We can therefore conclude there is no scientific proof that recently there is more snowfall. The focus should be not purely on the quantity of snowfall in a certain year, but more on the socio-economic impact of snowfall, which is different from the purely scientific perspective.

●**Measures to deal with snow in Tokyo**
From a disaster prevention perspective, it is vital to improve our capacity to forecast snow in Tokyo. On the other hand, for such events which only occur every once in a while, it seems difficult to rely on people's experience. In case of heavy snow in Tokyo, there is no need to evacuate, people could just wait home until things get under control. In such situations, the way people react is important, so from a disaster prevention and mitigation perspective a multifaceted approach is necessary.　(Hiroshi Takahashi)

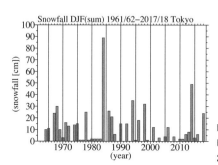

Fig. 1 Total depth of snow cover from December to February in Tokyo (1961/62– 2017/18)

Cumulus clouds along the Kampachi (ring road no. 8)

●**What kind of clouds?** The low clouds formed above the commonly-called Kampachi (the ring road no. 8, also metropolitan road 311) are well known. In meteorology, these are called fair weather cumulus clouds and they usually tend to form during clear summer days. As observation data are limited, the issue of these clouds has been debated as being one representative case of the influence of urbanization and human activities on the climate.

●**Under which atmospheric conditions do such clouds develop?** The fair weather cumulus clouds such as the Kampachi clouds usually are formed at altitudes of 1–2 km in the atmosphere. This is the atmospheric boundary layer (troposphere) whose upper limit is subject to the influence of the land surface, where the vapors condense and clouds are formed. More concretely, the land surface is heated by the solar radiation and its energy heats the lower layers of the atmosphere. Under the same pressure conditions, air gets lighter with increasing temperature, so that the warm air in the proximity of the land surface starts ascending (it acquires buoyancy). In fact, in the vicinity of the land surface, the air, while mixing, is gradually heated up from the lower layers upwards. The atmospheric layer under the influence of the land surface is the above-mentioned atmospheric boundary layer, which according to various conditions, is situated during summer at elevations of 1–2 km above Tokyo.

● **Inconsistency of location** Do such fair weather cumulus clouds form in the same area? Since they are named after the Kampachi, are they most often formed in this specific area? Actually, under conditions of clear weather during summer, similar cumulus clouds often occur in the Kanto mountain area. This is because from a thermodynamics perspective, mountains have a powerful effect and with differences in the daily wind flow, the influence of mountains is easy to notice. In Fig. 1, there are clouds above Izu Oshima. These can be also observed on other observation days. In the case of Izu Oshima, the sea breeze and the mountain breeze, 2 strong local winds, contribute to the formation of frequent clouds over the same area. So in order for clouds above the Kampachi to be formed frequently, there must be some strong conditioning factor at work. The influence of urbanization was thought to be such a factor, but observation data show that its impact is rather weak. As Fig. 1 shows, fair weather cumulus do not find conditions to be formed along the coast, they usually occur in inland areas. As a rule of thumb, since the Kampachi is inland from the coast, there is a higher probability to find fair weather cumulus in this area. What is interesting is that a survey on the frequency of cloud formation shows no trend of repeated fair weather cloud formation in the same area. The evidence shows that for the same area as in Fig. 1, 10–20 minutes time difference means the clouds are located in slightly different areas. Moreover, next day at the same time, the location is different.

●**Influence of urbanization?** With the progress of urbanization, the land surface cover has been changed, resulting in changes of its energy balance. The heat reaching the land surface is used for 2 purposes: to heat the land surface and for evaporation of soil humidity. With urbanization, the artificial land surface tends to be dry, so part of the heat which was used for evaporation is now used to overheat the land surface. However, the land surface is hotter all over Tokyo, not only in the Kampachi area, so that the influence of urbanization cannot explain the Kampachi clouds.

●Might it be a result of air pollution?

The link with air pollution and aerosols has also been debated. Aerosols are solid particles suspended in the atmosphere. A well-known example is the PM2.5. Not all of them are human-generated, there are some aerosols occurring naturally. Aerosols contribute not only to air pollution but also act as nuclei of condensation, contributing to the formation of clouds. With heavy traffic along Kampachi generating lots of aerosols, it might be assumed that these contribute to the creation of the Kampachi clouds, but at present we don't have enough data to establish their impact. Moreover, it is known that during Japan's high economic development period, air pollution in Tokyo was linked with a higher probability of cloud formation, but compared with the 1970s, the quantity of aerosols has diminished. The Kampachi clouds have been observed since the 1990s, so it is difficult to attribute them to air pollution.

●No direct link with heavy rainstorms

Another misconception is the one regarding the relation between the Kampachi clouds and local rainstorms; since Kampachi clouds are not rain-producing clouds, although there might be some relation between the weather conditions generating the Kampachi clouds and those generating heavy rainstorms, the link is not direct. While the Kampachi clouds phenomenon is difficult to explain scientifically, from a social perspective, it is a very important environmental issue. There are still many unknown impacts of urbanization and of the artificial land cover. Heatstroke, the impact on ecosystems, the problems related to aerosols, etc. are becoming major environmental problems.

(Hiroshi Takahashi)

Albedo Himawari8 VIS 500 nm

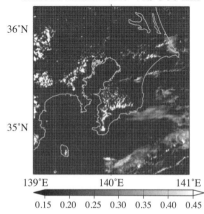

Fig.1 Albedo in Tokyo calculated based on data from meteorological satellite Himawari 8 (wavelength 500 nm)

The higher Albedo (in white) is due to cloud cover. Range of Albedo 0–1

Close-up

"Guerilla" torrential rains

●Definition of "guerilla" torrential rain

Every year in Tokyo, during the summer season, due to torrential precipitation—intense rain over a short interval of time—water from the sewer system overflows and we sometimes hear about water bursting from the manholes or about city roads being flooded. Urban surfaces are either covered in concrete or are building roof surfaces, so that when suddenly a huge quantity of rain falls, the water flows towards the sewage system and the river system in the area, concentrating towards the lower areas, and where the capacity to evacuate this water is not sufficient, flooding incidents occur.

During such incidents in 1999 (July 21) and 2008 (August 5), there were human victims and a few hundred facilities were totally or partially flooded. Due to the torrential rains' potential to cause blackouts or rail traffic to stop due to thunderbolt strikes, the impact on urban life is huge, so from a social perspective there is interest in this meteorological phenomenon. Chosen among the 10 top buzz words of 2008, guerilla torrential rain is defined as intense local rain caused by cumulonimbus clouds, and difficult to predict.

●The cumulonimbus clouds which generate torrential rains

The cumulonimbus clouds which generate short term torrential rains develop up to high altitudes, with the cloud top at over 10 km—at the upper boundary of the troposphere; each such cloud can have a diameter from few km to about 10 km. Tokyo's central wards area can be circumscribed in a circle with an approximate diameter of 30 km, so that while in some areas it's raining heavily, in other areas there is no rain at all (Fig. 1). Cumulonimbus clouds are short-lived, and intense rain only lasts from a few tens of minutes to 1 hour (Fig. 1). In order for cumulonimbus clouds to form, an ascendant/upward air flow is necessary, but once the torrential rain starts falling, a huge quantity of falling rain drops generate a descendant/downward air flow and after a while this slows down the formation of vapor feeding the cloud and producing raindrops. So once the torrential rain starts falling, the process of cloud dispersion also starts, leading to a rapid end. On the other hand, when the downward air flow reaches the land surface, it often forms remarkable horizontal wind divergence as a cold outflow. This cold air flow can uplift the warm air in its front side, and contributes to the formation of a new generation of cumulonimbus clouds.

●The urban influence

In urban areas, the land surface heats up due to the heat island effect, or due to the presence of high buildings the surface is uneven, both conditions for the formation of ascendant air currents in the lower layers of the atmosphere, leading to short intense rain episodes. It may be easy to speculate about such impacts, but actually, cumulonimbus clouds are also regularly formed in non-urban areas, so it is difficult to attribute torrential rains in urban areas to the impact of urbanization solely. Simulations also show that urbanization can have different effects: stimulating the formation of cumulonimbus clouds or the opposite process of dispersion. Research based on observation data relies on long time series of data from the network of observation of the quantity of precipitation or

Chapter 2 Tokyo's Climate ● *39*

from radar, or data on the regional character-istics of frequent torrential rain. Research shows that for metropolises in western countries, a maximum frequency area tends to appear in the 20–60 km leeward side of urban area, but in the Kanto area where the wind systems are very complicated, such trend is not yet elucidated (Ref. 1).

The area around the border of Tokyo/Saita-ma where the frequency of short torrential rains is higher (Fig. 2) tends to become a convergence zone between southerly winds dominating the central urban area and east-erly winds blowing in the southern area of Saitama Prefecture. In addition to the north-ern area of Tokyo, occurrence of short torren-tial rains is higher in the western and south-ern areas of Tokyo wards compared to the central and eastern areas.

(Hideo Takahashi)

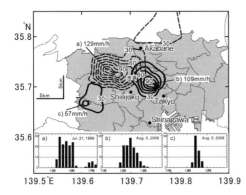

Fig. 1 Distribution of one hour accumulated precipitation amount and time sequence of ten minutes precipitation amount at the central areas of short torrential rains for two case studies (modified after Ref. 2)
July 21, 1999: dashed line and (a)
August 5, 2008: solid line and (b), (c)
Contour lines are drawn where the precipitation amount exceeds 30 mm/h (announcement criterion of JMA's heavy rain advisory for Tokyo wards area) at the interval of 15 mm/h. The gray area indicates the wards of the Tokyo Metropolis.

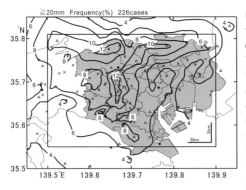

Fig. 2 Frequency distribution of short torrential rain (≧20 mm/h) in the urban core area of Tokyo (Ref. 3)
The values represent the percentage frequency calculated as a ratio of the number of cases of short torrential rain at each rain-gauge station to the total number of cases of short torrential rain that occurred in the box area within the figure (totaling 226 cases) during summer (June to September) of 1991–2012. The gray area indicates the wards of the Tokyo Metropolis.
●: AMeDAS station, △: JR station, ×: Tokyo Metropolis station.

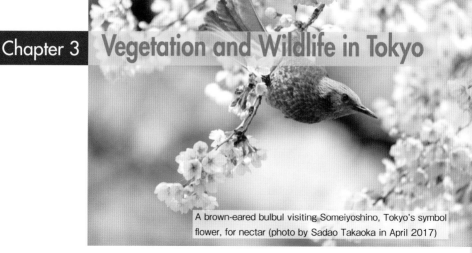

Chapter 3 Vegetation and Wildlife in Tokyo

A brown-eared bulbul visiting Someiyoshino, Tokyo's symbol flower, for nectar (photo by Sadao Takaoka in April 2017)

In Tokyo metropolitan area, there is precious nature that survived the destruction caused by urban development. There are natural areas which appear to have gradually recovered after Japan's period of high economic growth. On the other hand, due to the massive scale of land use changes and the penetration of invading alien species, some natural elements are disappearing. In the present chapter, we give a comprehensive overview of plants and animals as part of Tokyo's nature.

3.1 Diversity of forest vegetation

Tokyo's total area is not very broad, ranking 3rd from the bottom among Japan's 47 prefectures. However, the elevational span shows greater diversity, from Tokyo bay to the Mt. Kumotori in Okutama Town (2,017 m elevation), a span of approximately 2,000 m, raking 15th among all Japanese prefectures. Since Japan enjoys sufficient precipitation, the limiting factor for the distribution of vegetation is temperature, so that Tokyo, in spite of its limited area, has a great diversity of vegetation forms, due to its elevational span.

Focusing on the features of Tokyo's vegetation by elevation, firstly, in Tokyo's westernmost area, at elevations above 1,600 m around Mt. Kumotori, subalpine vegetation of evergreen coniferous forests (Fig. 3.1) is characteristic. Trees which cannot be seen in the lower areas, such as the black bark kometsuga (*Tsuga diversifolia*) or ash-color bark shirabiso (*Abies veitchii*), are representatives of the tall forest of Pinaceae tree species. During winter, the forest floor is covered with snow, but during summer there are low shrubbery trees such as koyoraku-tsutsuji (*Rhododendron pentandrum*) and azumashakunage (*Rhododendron degronianum*), and herbaceous, flowering species such as maizurusou (*Maianthemum dilatatum*), osabagusa (*Pteridophyllum racemosum*), baikaoren (*Coptis quinquefolia*).

In the elevational zone between approximately 700 m and 1,600 m, the cool temperate vegetation is characteristic. The natural forest is broadleaved deciduous forest of buna beech (*Fagus crenata*), mizunara oak (*Quercus crispula*) and maple species, admired for the fresh green in spring and for their fall colors. In the past, most of the natural vegetation of this elevational zone has been cleared and afterwards it either evolved through secondary succession to a secondary forest, or was replaced by plantations of sugi (Japanese cedar, *Cryptomeria japonica*) and hinoki (Japanese cypress, *Chamaecyparis obtusa*). In some spots the original climax forest (the forest evolved by natural primary succession to the highest final stage) still survives.

In the area surrounding Mt. Mito at the border with Yamanashi Prefecture, there is such a location where the climax forest can be observed (Fig. 3.2 left). On the mountain slopes the broadleaved deciduous forest with buna, inubuna (*Fagus japonica*), mizunara and maple species can be found, but on the ridges evergreen conifers such as tsuga (*Tsuga sieboldii*) and momi (*Abies firma*) are also present. Along the valley bottoms a distinctive forest vegetation including

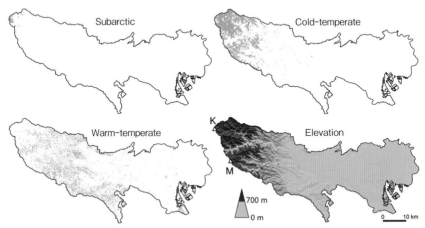

Fig. 3.1   Elevation and plant distribution in the mainland area of Tokyo.
Modified from the 1:25,000 vegetation map, GIS data released by the Biodiversity Center of Japan, Ministry of the Environment based on the 6th and 7th vegetation survey. The map covers the area of the climax forests and secondary vegetation. K = Mt. Kumotori, M = Mt. Mito Elevations are based on 10 meters mesh data released by the Geospatial Information Authority of Japan.

shioji (*Fraxinus platypoda*), sawagurumi (*Pterocarya rhoifolia*), katsura (*Cercidiphyllum japonicum*) can be observed, a riparian forest where occasional disturbance occurs under the impact of debris flows.

In this area of Mt. Mito there are big buna trees, but very few young trees or saplings to show natural regrowth. This demonstrates that the natural regeneration of the buna forest is not proceeding well, and it is assumed that in the future other deciduous species will replace it as main components of the forest (Ref. 1). While the forest appears unchanged to visitors, considering things at a longer time scale than that of human life, such changes are visible.

At elevations lower than 700 m, the warm temperate zone vegetation can be found. The climax forest for the warm temperate zone is the evergreen broadleaved forest, a mix of shii chinquapin species and kashi evergreen oak species, but in Tokyo it only survives in the island areas, while on mainland very little is left. However, in Tokyo's 23 wards there are some majestic forests created during and after the Edo period, very similar with the climax forests of the warm temperate climate. Such are those in the alluvial lowlands: Hama-rikyu Gardens (in Chuo Ward), Kiyosumi Gardens (in Koto Ward) consisting of sudajii (*Castanopsis sieboldii*) and tabunoki (*Machilus thunbergii*), resistant to the sea breeze, and on the uplands: Rikugien Gardens (in Bunkyo Ward), Shinjuku Gyoen National Garden (in Shinjuku Ward), Meiji Jingu shrine forest (in Shibuya Ward) etc. where old sudajii and evergreen oak species can be observed (Ref. 2). Especially Meiji Jingu's dense, luxuriant forest, would make one forget that it is located in the vicinity of Shinjuku's business district (see Close-up: Jingu's forest).

Fig. 3.2　Buna beech forest on Mt. Mito (left) and maruhachi, the arboreal fern found in the Ogasawara Islands (right) (Photos by Sadao Takaoka, left: in November 2018, right: in June 1995)

However, the most widespread type of natural forest to be found in Tokyo's warm temperate zone is the secondary broadleaved deciduous forest, dominated by konara oak (*Quercus serrata*) and kunugi oak (*Quercus acutissima*). In the past, such forests have been used for the production of charcoal and to provide compost for farming, and they are known under various names, such as *satoyama* or Musashino coppice woods. (see Close-up: *Satoyama*).

3.2   Tokyo's subtropical zone

As we mentioned above, in terms of area, Tokyo ranks 45th, while in terms of elevation span, 15th. When it comes to the north-south latitudinal span, it ranks first, since it includes Izu and Ogasawara Islands, with the southernmost Okinotorishima Island (Kitakojima, 20° 25′ 31″ N) separated from central Tokyo by more than 15 degrees of latitude and a distance of approximately 1,700 km. In the Ogasawara Islands, situated approximately 1,000 km south of the mainland, subtropical vegetation, not seen in Tokyo proper, can be found. One example of a subtropical plant widespread in the Ogasawara Islands is maruhachi (*Cyathea mertensiana*), an arboreal fern which grows taller than human stature (Fig. 3.2 right).

On Ogasawara Islands' Chichijima and Hahajima Islands, although at approximately the same latitude as Okinawa's main island, the climate is different (Ref. 3). Average annual precipitation in Naha City in Okinawa Prefecture (1981 –2010) is 2,041 mm, compared with Chichijima where it is 1,293 mm, and when the Ogasawara anticyclone takes over during summer (June–September), the amount of precipitation is only about half that of Naha City. Some of the dominant species in Ogasawara are shimaisunoki (*Distylium lepidotum*) and muninhimetsubaki (*Schima wallichii* subsp. mertensiana), both dwarf xerophytic shrubs, representative for the local climate (Ref. 3). However, the islands' climate and vegetation vary with elevation. On Hahajima Island, in the area of Mt. Chibusa (463 m), the clouds tend to gather around the peak. In this area wadannoki (*Dendrocacalia crepidifolia*) and other epiphytes such as shimaootaniwatari (*Asplenium nidus*) can be found, characteristic for the cloud forest.

Most of the plants we introduced in this section are endemic species. In the Ogasawara Islands, which have never been linked with the continental mass, the species of plants and animals, carried by ocean currents or by birds, had to adapt and evolve, so the rate of endemic species is very high.   Although the subtropical landscapes created by these species, different from the ones on the mainland, are quite far from the imagination of most people, these are also landscapes which make Tokyo proud.

3.3 Wild birds in Tokyo

Due to their natural caution or to the peculiarities of their habitat, the opportunities to observe wildlife are very limited in Tokyo, but birds are comparatively more visible.   Sparrows (*Passer montanus*), grey starlings (*Spodiopsar cineraeus*), brown-eared bulbul (*Hypsipetes amaurotis*), oriental turtle doves (*Streptopelia orientalis*) etc.   are some of the species populating the urban areas with sparse greenery.

For the distribution of bird species in Tokyo, we rely on data of a survey that has been carried continuously since the 1970s (Ref. 4), according to which the Japanese pygmy woodpecker (*Dendrocopos kizuki*) (Fig. 3.3 left) and the Japanese white eye (*Zosterops japonicus*) can reproduce even in very limited green areas, and are proliferating in the lower plain areas of Tokyo.   Recently, even forest birds, such as the varied tit (*Poecile varius*) or narcissus flycatcher (*Ficedula narcissina*) are expanding their habitats.   Moreover, birds of prey such as the Japanese sparrowhawk (*Accipiter gularis*) were found to be nesting in green plots surrounded by dense residential areas (Fig. 3.3 center).   The reason for which birds previously difficult to observe in Tokyo's urbanized lowlands are

Fig. 3.3 A Japanese pygmy woodpecker kogera feeding in a park tree (left), a Japanese sparrow hawk resting in the trees of a residential area (center), a Siberian meadow bunting in the grass along the Tama River (all photos by Sadao Takaoka, left: in January 2015, center: in May 2016, right: in April 2018)

now increasingly visible is perhaps the fact that Tokyo's green areas have improved. Coppice woods which in the past used to be cleared periodically have developed into mature forests, planted trees in parks and along avenues have matured. While the total area of forest and greenery has been diminishing in Tokyo over the past 100 years, the quality of green space as habitat for bird species has improved.

On the other hand, open field/open forest species such as bull-headed shrike (*Lanius bucephalus*) and skylark (*Alauda arvensis*) diminished in numbers. Due to the expansion of residential areas, the area of farmland fields has dropped, while the conversion of grain fields (habitat for open field bird species), to vegetable fields has also meant the habitat destruction for such birds. Birds found along rivers, such as the Siberian meadow bunting (*Emberiza cioides*) (Fig. 3.3 right) are also diminishing in numbers.

3.4 Protagonists of Tokyo's nights: mammals

We sometime hear news about raccoons showing up in the urban areas of Tokyo and being captured by the police or the fire departments. Such mammals active at night are a rare sight, but they live surprisingly close to us (see Close up: Tokyo's raccoon dogs).

We take a look at a survey of mammal species in Hamura City, one of Tokyo's suburbs (Ref. 5). The survey, conducted over 13 months starting in July 2017 and based on the recordings of an automatic photo camera set along the Tama River's floodplain, recorded raccoon dogs (*Nyctereutes procyonoides*), wild boars (*Sus scrofa*), alien raccoons (*Procyon lotor*), Japanese hares (*Lepus brachyurus*), Japanese marten (*Martes melampus*), Japanese weasel (*Mustela itatsi*), masked

Fig. 3.4 Wild boar (left) and raccoon (right) photographed at night with an automatic camera (both photos by Sadao Takaoka, left: in August 2017, right: in March 2018)

palm civet (*Paguma larvata*), red fox (*Vulpes vulpes*), Japanese badger (*Meles anakuma*), Pallas' squirrel (*Callosciurus erythraeus*) etc. (Fig. 3.4). Raccoon dogs were recorded daily, wild boar and alien raccoons over 100 times. This frequency is perhaps explained by the location of the camera in the proximity of the Kusabana Hills, which means that the mammals in the area have habitats ranging from the hill forests to the open grassland. While they hide during the day in the forest and shrubbery, they roam freely at night. But what is the situation in the residential areas, where there is far less nature than along the Tama River? If we take a look at the survey of bodies of mammals that died naturally or were killed in accidents on the roads or on residential properties, Japanese and alien raccoons, civets, foxes, wild boars and weasels were recorded. It seems that in Hamura city, where rapid residential and industrial development occurred after World War II, these animals continue to survive unbeknown to people.

When we consider Tokyo's western mountain area, there are bigger mammals, not found in the lower areas, such as the Asiatic black bear (*Ursus thibetanus*), sika deer (*Cervus nippon*), Japanese serow (*Capricornis crispus*), Japanese macaque (*Macaca fuscata*) etc. These mammals were pushed towards the western mountain areas due to the urban offensive and to hunting, but since about the 1980s, their numbers started recovering and the damages to farming and forestry also increased. For example, in 1992 the sika deer population was limited to the area of Okutama Town, but it has been expanding its area eastwards ever since, and in 2015 they were found in Hinohara Village, Ome, Akiruno, Hachioji Cities, and the western area of Hinode Town (Ref. 6).

The impact of the increasing population of sika deer on the natural vegetation is significant. In the area of Okutama, due to grazing by deer, the forest floor vegetation has receded, and the forest is now dominated by plants not favored by deer such as warabi (*Pteridium aquilinum* var. *latiusculum*) and marubadakebuki (*Ligularia dentata*) which prosper. In some areas, due to overgrazing, slope denudation occurs, which can lead to soil erosion on the steeper slopes.

3.5   Nature along Tama River

Crossing the Metropolis in its upper and middle course and forming the boundary with Kanagawa Prefecture in the lower course, the Tama River still conserves greenery along its banks, providing Tokyo's urban dwellers with

Fig. 3.5   Kawaranogiku Aster in bloom (left) and long-billed plover and chicks on the floodplain (both photos by Sadao Takaoka, left: in October 2015, right: in May 2016)

space for recreation, walks and fishing etc.

Tama River's water quality deteriorated during Japan's high economic growth period, with BOD (biochemical oxygen demand) measurements at Chofu sampling station (13 km upriver from the river mouth) showing over 10 mg/L, considered a limit to the survival of fish.   With the expansion of water infrastructure, the quality of water gradually improved, so that after the year 2000, BOD measurements constantly show approximately 2 mg/L (Ref. 7).   As a result, the ayu sweetfish (which disappeared in the late 1960s to 1970s) can be observed again swimming up the river.

However, changes occurring along the Tama River are not limited to the water. Kawaranogiku (*Aster kantoensis*), a plant widespread in the middle course of the river in the past, has seen its habitat diminishing, and was thought to be threatened with extinction.   Currently, limited patches of it can be found along the river in Fussa, Hamura, Akiruno Cities.   Why did such a thing happen? The floodplain is made up of pebbles and sand, with low water retention capacity; furthermore, it can get very hot and dry due to direct solar radiation, so this is a difficult environment for plants, similar with desert conditions.   Besides, whenever flooding occurs, the area is submerged, so it is a very unstable environment for plants.   In the floodplain, along with the above mentioned aster, there are other plants such as kawarasaiko (*Potentilla chinensis*), kawarayomogi (*Artemisia capillaris*), kawaraketsumei (*Chamaecrista nomame*), which all include *kawara* ("river bank") in their names, all of them riparian plants adapted to survive in this difficult environment of the flood plain, which changes during each flood with the accumulation of new alluvium (Ref. 8).   Due to the building of dams to prevent floods and to the extraction of sand during the Showa era, the river channel has become entrenched, so that the higher banks are not much affected by flooding. As a consequence, in the higher floodplain vegetation succession has occurred, with grass and trees taking over. The shorter plants mentioned above are losing the competition with taller plants such as ogi (*Miscanthus sacchariflorus*) or susuki (*Miscanthus sinensis*). The floodplain has been also taken over by forests of alien species, such as harienju (*Robinia pseudoacacia*), or some areas have been converted to sports grounds, which further diminish the habitat of the riparian species. The impact that these vegetation changes have on the wildlife has been also noticed. Different vegetation, in terms of height or density of plants, has a direct impact on Orthoptera species in the area, but for kawarabatta (*Eusphingonotus japonicus*), the Orthoptera specific to the areas of the floodplain covered with gravel, the situation is severe since they are losing their habitat, and as a result have been registered on Tokyo's red list (Ref. 9).

A similar situation is that of birds nesting on sand and gravel in the lower sector of the floodplain, such as koajisashi (*Sterna albifrons*) and chidori (*Charadrius* spp.) (Fig. 3.5), also found on Tokyo's red list. As the previously widespread reed fields are also diminishing, birds reproducing in such areas as ōyoshikiri (great reed warble, *Acrocephalus orientalis*) or sekka (fan-tailed warbler, *Cisticola juncidis*) are also threatened. Floods negatively affect vegetation and change the landforms, so that the impact on vegetation and wildlife is huge, but in the floodplain there is vegetation in various stages of succession, so the floodplain offers diverse habitats and environments, and in the long run the disturbance caused by flooding is a necessary process for the living organisms along the Tama River.

3.6 Changing wildlife

As we showed in the previous paragraphs, there are species threatened with extinction and species with diminishing habitats, but on the other hand, some other species have been expanding their habitats in recent years. One example is the araiguma raccoon mentioned above, a non-native species. It was first introduced in the late 1970s, as a popular pet imported from America, but following its release in the wild it has become feral and spread all over the country. It looks quite cute, but since it damages the ecosystem and farming operations, it was put on the list of alien species, according to the Invasive Alien Species Act.

Fig. 3.6 Hwamei singing in the bush (left) and Indian fritillary (right) (both photos by Sadao Takaoka; left: in July 2018, right: in October 2017)

Among the bird species introduced by humans, there are more than 20 species established in Tokyo, and except for the species with a long history, systematically introduced like the dobato (*Columba livia*) and kojukei (*Bambusicola thoracicus*) for hunting, most of the alien species were those initially introduced as pets after 1960s, which escaped in the wild. Among the registered species is gabicho (Hwamei, *Garrulax canorus*) (Fig. 3.6 left), established in Tokyo since around the 1990s, initially in the mountain and hilly areas, but recently expanding in the urban area (Ref. 10). Gabicho prefers thickets and *Sasa* bamboo bushes for feeding and reproducting grounds, and in Tokyo its song can be heard from spring to summer.

There are also species which expanded their habitat to Tokyo from other regions of Japan. Among the species of butterflies, nagasakiageha (great mormon butterfly, *Papilio memnon*) and tsumagurohyomon (Indian fritillary, *Argyreus hyperbius*) (Fig. 3.6 right), 2 southern species, are present in Tokyo since around 2000 (Ref. 11). With such species expanding their habitat northward, climate change seems to be the main cause, however there might be other causes involved. For example, in the case of tsumagurohyomon (Indian fritillary, *Argyreus hyperbius*), they feed on pansies and other garden plants, so their eggs and larvae might have been transported by people.

On the other hand, a species of similar southern origin, the akaboshigomadara (red ring skirt, *Hestina assimilis*), which is of Chinese origin and has been released here, has spread since the 1990s in the southern area of Kanto, and since the late 2000s there have been sightings in Tokyo (Ref. 10). Currently it has naturalized and can be found all around Kanto, being also registered as an alien species.

(Sadao Takaoka)

Jingu's forest

●**Solemn green island in the middle of the city** Meiji Jingu's shrine forest, exuberantly growing west of the Harajuku Station on Yamanote Line, was planted during the Taisho era in honor of the Meiji Emperor. It is one of Tokyo's representative cultural landmarks, but at the same time, nowadays with its good accessibility it is one of the valuable places to understand Tokyo's nature (Fig. 1). Seen on an aerial photograph, this wide and thick forest is a very special presence in the center of the city. The forest continues to evolve, and recently its dense canopy has become visible from the top of the taller buildings in the area (Fig. 2).

●**The creation of Jingu's forest** The creation of Jingu's forest goes back to the Taisho period. On topographical maps and in photographical documents of the time, the area now under Jingu's forest used to be covered by a coppice wood (secondary forest) dominated by pines and grassland. Jingu's forest was planned on this land by forestry experts such as Seiroku Honda, who envisioned a combination of slowly growing species, able to withstand urban pollution and develop into a stately forest (Ref. 1).

According to their vision, the main species chosen for the forest were oaks, chinquapins and camphors, all evergreen, broadleaved, tall-growing tree species. These evergreen broadleaved species are also called lucidophyllous species, for the deep green color of their glossy thick leaves even during winter. These lucidophyllous species are very strong to air pollution and in a suitable habitat they develop into a stable forest over time. At the time, trees were donated from all over Japan and many trees of lucidophyl-

lous species were planted.

However, Tokyo is located at the northern boundary of these species' natural habitat, therefore the speed of development has been very slow. Planting only slowly developing lucidophyllous species from the beginning would have meant that for a while, the forest would look sparse, not suitable as Jingu's forest. The solution found was to keep the already extant tall pine trees and underneath them to sparsely plant evergreen conifers such as hinoki (Japanese cypress: *Chamaecyparis obtuse*) and sugi (Japanese cedar: *Cryptomeria japonica*) and finally, the lucidophyllous tree species, expected to become the protagonists in the future, were planted in the lowest layer. So the initial vision was to plant species with different growth speed, in the expectation that by the time the conifers would succumb to competition, the slowly-growing lucidophyllous species would be in their prime, protagonists of a stately forest. Nowadays, almost 100 years later, Jingu's forest stands majestic and quiet, result of this impressive vision and planning process.

●**Natural environment of Jingu's forest**

Nowadays, we can admire Jingu's forest, where lucidophyllous species develop in a semi-natural state (Ref. 2). These lucidophyllous forests naturally develop mainly in Kyushu and other areas of western Japan, with the Kanto Plain and Tohoku's coastal areas as the northern boundary of their natural habitat (Ref. 3). At this northern boundary, in the Kanto Plain, in the past, these species have been replaced with other deciduous species such as konara oaks etc., (which lose their leaves during winter and are useful for charcoal making and firewood) and red pines, resulting in secondary coppice woods. Most of these coppice woods have been abandoned after the so called "energy/fuel revolution" which occurred around 1960, but they continue to develop. Jingu's forest, by comparison, has been evolving for the past 100 years and is now close to the natural state of a lucidophyllous forest.

These are the specific features of Jingu's forest, visible from the main sanctuary and the path to the shrine. On the other hand, the south-western park area of the Jingu forest, called the Gyoen, is a totally different type of forest (Fig. 3). This is not a lucidophyllous forest, but one consisting of broadleaved deciduous species, such as konara oaks, inushide Carpinus species, colorful maples, which turn in fall. It is assumed that this is a remnant of the coppice woods that used to cover this area. At the same time, the Gyoen area conserves intact the initial landforms, such as the shallow valleys which cut through the Yodobashi Uplands, a very precious landscape.

(Tatsuhiro Isogai)

Fig. 1 Evergreen broadleaved dense forest of the shrine, which remains green during winter. (photo by Tatsuhiro Isogai in February 2019)

Fig. 2 Jingu's exuberant forest seen from Tokyo Metropolitan Government Building. (photo by Tatsuhiro Isogai in April 2019)

Fig. 3 In the Gyoen, deciduous broadleaved forests are seen on the initial landforms of the Yodobashi Uplands in the Gyoen. (photo by Tatsuhiro Isogai in February 2019)

Satoyama

●*Satoyama* **as nature** Nature surrounding villages, which used to support rural communities' life is named *satoyama*. *Satoyama* consists of the secondary forests and grasslands regenerated after repeated clearings and fire, or, in a broader context, it includes the paddies and fields, the irrigation ponds and channels, the forests surrounding shrines, temples and residences, the whole rural landscape. Fig. 1 shows a *satoyama* landscape located in Onoji area, Machida City. The forest surrounds the farm fields, and from the colors and the different density of canopy, it is obvious that the forest consists of a mix of various broadleaved deciduous species. Despite suffering for a long time repeated human-caused disturbance, these forests show a high biodiversity, result of appropriate degree of human disturbance generating a mosaic of natural conditions, which in turn act as diverse habitats and environments for more diverse vegetation and wildlife .

●**Origins of the coppice woods** Tama area's *satoyama* secondary forests consist of a mix of broadleaved deciduous species such as kunugi (*Quercus accutissima*), konara (*Quercus serrata*), shide (*Carpinus* spp.) and are called coppice woods. Nowadays, these survive mainly in mountain and hilly areas, but until the 1970s, they used to cover the flat areas of the uplands as well. The uplands have been gradually encroached by suburbanization and currently very few patches of the original coppices remain.

In the past, they used to provide firewood and charcoal, as well as the organic compost needed by rural households. This means these coppice woods were managed according to a 10 to 20 years cycle, the tree branches being regularly trimmed and the forest floor kept clean (mowing the grass, raking the dead leaves).

The main tree species in the coppice woods are those that after each cutting regenerate from the stump and sprout new branches. This characteristic explains the fact that after repeated clearing the forest could be used continuously. The new branches are those usually dormant, stimulated to grow after the main trunk has been cut. Walking in a coppice wood, the specific shape of the trees can be observed: from the root, there are multiple trunks developing independently, almost parallel (Fig. 2).

This is proof that regular tree cutting and sprouting has been practiced. Since around 1960, the use of coppice woods has been abandoned. Fig. 3 shows the shift away from firewood and charcoal to coal, at national level and later to oil, electricity and gas, which became the main sources of energy for most households. Even in Tokyo, the production of charcoal declined from 13,389 t in 1956 to less than 100 t currently (Ref. 1). With organic compost being replaced by chemical fertilizers, the regular grass mowing and raking of leaves was also abandoned.

●**Changes of** *satoyama* In the abandoned coppice woods, there are different changes occurring. In the coppice woods of the hills in the Tama area, most trees are nowadays about 20 m high. If we compare this with the situation in the first half of Meiji Era, using the military surveillance data, we notice that at that time the *satoyama* forest in the Kanto area was dominated by oaks

(*Quercus* spp.) mostly less than 4 m high (Ref. 2). Furthermore, if we look at the results of the vegetation survey conducted from 1969 to 1985 in Tokyo and the surrounding area, they also show that most trees are less than 10 m high, with some less than 5 m high (Refs. 3, 4). The regular thinning and clearing ceased more than 50 years ago, so the coppice woods had the time to develop into mature forests.

The changes are not only manifest in the height of the forest, but also in its composition, with shirakashi (*Quercus myrsinfolia*), arakashi (*Quercus glauca*), hisakaki (*Eurya japonica* var. *japonica*), aoki (*Aucuba japonica* var. *japonica*) etc., evergreen broadleaved species proliferating in the lower shrub layer, while on the forest floor species like azu-

manezasa (*Pleioblastus chino*) grow densely. Alien bird species populating the thickets such as gabicho (*Garrulax canorus*) (Chapter 3, Fig. 3.6)—a species imported since the Edo period (Ref. 5) and probably escaped or released since those times, have recently multiplied, a fact that might be related to the recent densification of *satoyama* forest. Another change taking place all over the country is the expansion of bamboo groves. In Fig. 1 (left side of the picture), mousouchiku bamboo (*Phyllostachys edulis*) can be identified expanding among the broadleaved tree species. The expansion of bamboo groves is so significant that it is feared it is going to alter the entire *satoyama* landscape.

(Sadao Takaoka)

Fig. 1 *Satoyama* in Onoji area, Machida City (photo by Sadao Takaoka in December 2018)

Fig. 2 A stump of konara oak tree with multiple ramifications (photo by Sadao Takaoka in December 2018)

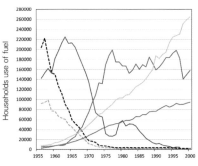

--- fuel wood (100 m³ stacked)   --- charcoal (10 t)
— coal (1000 t)   — oil (kl)
— electricity (million kwh)   — urban gas (billion kcal)

Fig. 3 Changes in the national households use of fuel (modified from Japan Gas Association "Synopsis of Gas Business". Data for fuel wood and charcoal represent production, data for coal, oil and urban gas represent quantity sold, and for electricity the quantity used. Data up to 1997 represent annual data, after 1998 data for fiscal year.

Tokyo's raccoon dogs

●Raccoon dogs in Tokyo? In Tokyo's Nerima Ward, there is a sign along the road reading "Warning: wildlife" (Fig. 1) and showing something resembling a raccoon dog (*Nyctereutes procyonoides*); is it possible that raccoon dogs would show up in this area? It might be that the warning designates not only the raccoon dog, but also the common raccoon (*Procyon lotor*), masked palm civet (*Paguma larvata*) and other medium-size wild mammals, which live in the area and might cross the road. In the area there is a large park and some small size farm fields, so this might constitute a favorable habitat for these mammals.

This means that while Tokyo's continuous urbanization might have reduced the habitat of wildlife, it did not totally wipe it out. Sightings of animals such as the raccoon dog, which for a while disappeared from Tokyo, are now again confirmed.

After World War II, significant land use changes occurred in Tokyo (Ref. 1). At the beginning of the 1930s, except for the central area of the city (overlapping the urban area of Edo), the surroundings were still covered by greenery (forests, grasslands, farmland, parks), but by the mid-1960s most of the urban areas of the special wards have lost their green areas. The raccoon dogs, red foxes (*Vulpes vulpes*), Japanese weasels (*Mustela itatsi*) which in the 1920s had their habitat even in the area of Tokyo's wards, were pushed gradually towards the west, with their distribution reduced to mountain areas west of Hachioji City in the 1970s. Since the 1990s though, sightings of raccoon dogs have been increasingly reported in the suburban green areas and residential areas, and since the 2000s, even in central areas such as the Imperial Palace, Akasaka Imperial Grounds, National Park for Nature Study or Shinjuku Gyoen National Garden, becoming a frequent sight in the green areas of the central wards. According to a survey of Urban Wildlife Institute (Ref. 2), in the interval 2001-June 2007, there have been sightings of raccoon dogs in 21 wards (all except the Chuo and Sumida Wards).

Genetic research on the origin of these raccoon dogs continues, to elucidate whether they disappeared and then came to repopulate these areas from the surrounding areas or they somehow survived development in this area and see a recent revival (Ref. 3).

●The urban life of raccoon dogs The author teaches at a university in Tama area of Kawasaki City, in the suburbs of Tokyo, and sometimes, in the early morning or in the evening has had the opportunity to see raccoon dogs either on campus or in the residential areas surrounding it (Fig. 2). However, in day time it is very rare to see raccoon dogs, because they are night animals. They are considered omnivores, but what is it that they find to feed on at night in these residential areas?

An analysis of the contents of raccoon dog droppings on the campus of Tsuda University in Kodaira City (Ref. 4) has shown that in spring these contain remains of animal protein, in summer remains of insects and leaves, in fall fruit and seeds, so their food varies according with the season. Among the animal remains, beetles, snails, birds' feathers, mammal hair etc. could be identified, so it seems raccoon dogs feed on the animals near the earth surface and perhaps even carcasses. Among the plants identified were seeds of mukudori tree (*Aphananthe aspera*), persimmon (*Diospyros kaki*), enoki tree (*Celtis sinensis*), ginkgo tree (*Ginkgo biloba*), dwarf lily turf (*Ophiopogon japonicus*), mainly plants found in the green urban areas. Traces of rubber, plastic, aluminium foil, polystyrene have been also identified.

Analysis of the stomach contents of dead raccoon dogs found in a residential area of Kawasaki brings additional details on the feeding habits of urban raccoon dogs. According to the survey in Kawasaki (Ref. 5) such food included rice, noodles, vegetables, fried eggs etc., leftovers; in some instances, only dog food or only noodles and sausages were found. Therefore, raccoon dogs not only feed on what is available in the green urban areas, but also rely on leftovers they collect from the garbage or on pet food available around homes.

●**Raccoon dogs' fate**   Actually, most of the raccoon dogs corpses analyzed for the survey mentioned above were killed on the road, due to car accidents. Such traffic accidents involving wildlife are called road kills. For urban raccoon dogs, there might be ways of finding food in this urban environment, but this comes at a price. The signs we mentioned at the beginning of this chapter, warning of raccoon dogs, should better read "Warning: cars" to warn the raccoon dogs themselves. We should also promote more wildlife-friendly roads and driving habits.

(Sadao Takaoka)

Fig. 1   A sign along the road in Nerima Ward reading "Warning: wildlife" (photo by Sadao Takaoka in February 2019)

Fig. 2   A raccoon dog appearing in a residential area early in the morning (photo by Sadao Takaoka in December 2018)

Chapter 4 Tokyo's Waters and Seas

Entrance of Tokyo Bay seen from "Ogasawara-maru" that connects central Tokyo and Ogasawara (Bonin) Islands. The land on the right is Sunozaki, Boso Peninsula (photo by Hiroshi Matsuyama in February 2018)

Ever since Tokugawa Ieyasu founded Edo, securing fresh water has been a vital issue for the city; currently, approximately 80% of the water used in Tokyo is provided by the Tone and Ara River systems. On the other hand, Tokyo administers over 45% of the sea waters under Japanese jurisdiction. When considering vital marine resources such as minerals and the fisheries, the crucial role of Tokyo's island areas becomes obvious.

4.1 Tokyo's waters

Tokyo's rivers The rivers flowing through Tokyo can be classified as class A rivers (92 of them, among which the Tama, Ara, Tone, and Tsurumi River systems), and class B rivers (15 of them), overall 107 rivers (Fig. 4.1). The total length of these rivers amounts to 858 km, of which, with the exception of rivers managed by the Land and Infrastructure Ministry, Tokyo Metropolitan Government manages 711 km (Ref. 1).

Tama River has its sources in Yamanashi Prefecture, around Mt. Kasatori, and flows through the Okutama Lake, after which it receives a number of tributaries such as the Aki and Asa Rivers and it finally flows into Tokyo Bay near Haneda in Ota Ward. Ara River has its sources in Mt. Kobushigatake, around the border area of Saitama, Yamanashi and Nagano Prefectures and it flows through the Chichibu Basin and the Nagatoro gorges before entering the Kanto Plain; here, it takes a southern direction and flows into Tokyo Bay forming the border between the Koto and Edogawa Wards. Sumida River diverges from it in Kita Ward. Edo River belongs to the Tone River system. In the past, the Tone River used to flow into Tokyo Bay, but during the Edo period, it was redirected towards east, to

Choshi in Chiba Prefecture where it flows into the ocean (Fig. 4 of Introduction). Edo River diverges from the Tone River in the area of Goka town in Ibaraki Prefecture and Noda City in Chiba Prefecture. It flows south, and after passing Ichikawa City in Chiba Prefecture, it separates into the Edo River and Kyu Edo River. Tsurumi River has its source in Machida City and flows eastwards reaching the Tokyo Bay in Yokohama's Tsurumi Ward. All the rivers mentioned

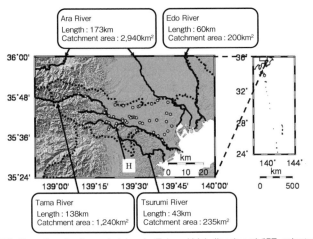

Fig. 4.1 Distribution of main rivers draining in Tokyo (thick lines) and "57 selected springs in Tokyo" (dots). The dashed lines depict the boundary of Tokyo Metropolis and surrounding prefectures, overlain on the landform map. "H" indicates the position of the springs draining near Hino City's Central Library (Fig. 4.4).

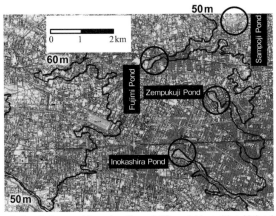

Fig. 4.2 Four ponds located around the elevation of 50 m at Musashino Uplands, edited from the landform map 1:25,000 "Kichijoji". Thick lines respectively show 50 m and 60 m of the elevation.

above are class A rivers.

Although many rivers flow through Tokyo, the history of Tokyo has been always linked with the efforts to secure fresh water. As we already explained in Chapter 1, the Musashino Uplands in western Tokyo is covered with thick layers of volcanic ash (Kanto loam) so precipitation infiltrates rapidly into the ground and water used to be less accessible. On the other hand, in the lowlands, wells only find water with a high content of salt, so the quality of water is not good. In the past, Tokyo had difficulties in securing fresh water.

Ponds originating in springs around the elevation of 50 m   Tracing the 50 m contour line on the landform map 1:25,000 "Kichijoji", we discover an interesting fact (Fig. 4.2). On this map, in the south, Inokashira Pond, Zempukuji Pond, Fujimi Pond are all situated along the 50 m contour line. Furthermore, to the north, Sampoji Pond is situated close to the elevation of 47.5 m. The fact that all these 4 ponds are situated at approximately the same elevation is not a random occurrence, and in the past, they shared sources in the natural springs of the Musashino Uplands.

Musashino Uplands is covered with very thick layers of volcanic ash, originating in the past eruptions of volcanoes such as Mt. Fuji and Mt. Hakone, situated west from Tokyo. This is why these layers are thicker in the western area and thin out eastwards. Tokyo's natural springs can be classified into two categories: the valley head type and the cliff line type (Fig. 4.3), with the first type usually developing on the surface of the plateau in natural horseshoe depressions, and the second type occurring at the foot of the cliff line. All 4 of the ponds mentioned above used to have sources in springs of the valley head type, although due to human activity, currently the springs are not active any longer. That is, the relation between the thickness of the volcanic ash layer and

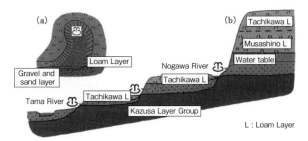

Fig. 4.3   Schematic diagram of draining springs (based on Ref. 2).
(a) the valley head type, (b) the cliff line type

the position of the groundwater is determinant for the location of springs. In the eastern area of the Musashino Uplands, this location is approximately the elevation of 50 m.

Tokyo's natural springs   Let's take another look at Fig. 4.2. In the lower left corner of the map, the contour lines marking 50 m and 60 m are concentrated in one area. This irregular distribution of the contour lines reflects the presence of a cliff line in the area. This is called the Kokubunji Cliff Line and natural springs occur at the foot of the cliff.

Musashino Uplands was created as an alluvial fan by the Tama River during the last glaciation, and on top of the gravel and sand layers lay thick layers of volcanic ash. Since the volcanic ash has very good permeability for water, precipitation penetrates to the underground gravel and sand layers (Fig. 4.3b). Usually, on alluvial fans, each time when flooding occurs, the river changes its channel so that it erodes the alluvium of the fan, creating a river terrace. In the section of the cliff of the terrace, the layers of gravel and sand are exposed, and this is where natural springs can be observed. This means that the Kokubunji Cliff Line was created when the Tama River flowed northeast from its current position.

Recently, natural springs are the focus of new interest from a conservation perspective. In 2013, in the Tokyo Metropolis (including the islands) a number of 616 springs were recorded (Ref. 2). Tokyo Metropolitan Government, aiming to conserve the springs, has designated "57 selected springs in Tokyo" in 2003

Fig. 4.4   The springs draining near Hino City's Central Library, one of the "57 selected springs in Tokyo" (photo by Hiroshi Matsuyama in February, 2008)

(Fig. 4.1).   Among the selection criteria water quantity, quality, origin of the springs, surrounding landscape were considered.   Fig 4.4 shows one of these, the springs draining near Hino City's Central Library (designated on the map as H in Fig. 4.1).   Since these springs originate in the precipitation infiltrating the underground, they need conservation.   The local governments of the area located on top of the cliff provide water-permeable pavements and trenches for the infiltration of precipitation, actively promoting the infiltration of the precipitation in the underground.

Tokyo's water resources   Let's reconsider Tokyo's water resources based on Fig. 4.1.   In the lower left area, the boundary between Kanagawa and Yamanashi Prefectures is the familiar type, marked by a water divide or by a river channel; on the other hand, the border between Tokyo Metropolis and the Yamanashi Prefecture, west of Ogochi Dam Lake is somehow unusual.   This is a reflection of the efforts to secure water resources during Meiji era, when Tokyo repeatedly merged with local administrations in the area, continuously expanding westward (Ref. 3).

The construction of Okutama Lake (Ogochi Dam) was completed in 1957, and at the time it was thought that it would provide Tokyo with plentiful water resources.   However, in August 1964, the year of the first Tokyo Olympics, the water level in the lake dropped by 100 m due to severe drought.   During the high economic development period, Tokyo's population dramatically increased, so that the efforts to secure water intensified.   Nowadays, approximately 20% of the water used in Tokyo is provided by the Tama River system while the remaining 80% comes from the Tone and Ara River systems.

The importance of surface water for various uses is obvious, but in Tokyo most of the fresh water for human consumption comes from underground sources. The groundwater in Tokyo's lowlands is unsuitable for drinking but in spite of its salinity, it can be used for industrial and agricultural purposes.   It is enough to dig a deep well and the groundwater springs out; cheap and convenient, it has been used for various purposes.   However the geological layers in this lowland area are soft, and since the beginning of the 20th century, the process of land subsidence continues (Ref. 4).   This is caused by the over-pumping of groundwater which leads to its level to drop, and the geological layers, mainly the clay, to contract.   The consequence is the process of building protrusion in which the foundations of buildings protrude from the ground.   In order to access the entrance, additional stairs are needed.

Following the adoption of the law of industrial water management, regulations regarding water use for business buildings, and those regarding water withdrawal were enforced. The situation of land subsidence improved since the 1970s. However, after that, the level of groundwater recovered to previous one and a reverse process known as "floating" can be observed for underground structures (such as Tokyo and Ueno Stations' underground platforms). As a measure to prevent this process, underground structures are loaded with more weight, and the groundwater is pumped to be used for industry and other purposes.

 ## 4.2 Tokyo's seas

Tokyo: A marine empire   Japan is an island country surrounded by the sea (Fig. 4.5), and there are so many islands in the sea. The northernmost territory is Etorofu Island, the westernmost is Yonaguni Island, the southernmost is Okinotorishima Island, while the easternmost is Minamitorishima Island, with the last two belonging to Ogasawara Village, part of Tokyo Metropolis.

In the following section, we are going to explain some of the terms used in Fig. 4.5, based on Ref. 5-8. The territorial sea is the marine belt surrounding the

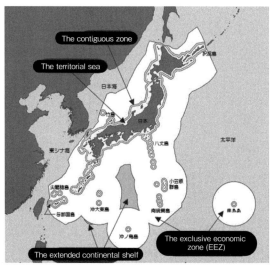

Fig. 4.5 Schematic diagram of the territorial sea and other related terms around Japan (modified after Ref. 5)

coast of a country (in this case, Japan), extending 12 marine miles (approximately 22 km; 1 marine mile corresponds to 1.852 km) counting from the baseline (the coastline at the lowest tide).   The contiguous zone is a belt outside of the terrestrial sea, expanding 24 marine miles away from the coast.   Here, access by foreign ships is controlled under the coastal country's jurisdiction.   The exclusive economic zone (EEZ) is a belt 200 marine miles wide (approximately 370 km), outwards of the territorial sea, including the sea floor and the underground of it.   Here, a country has exclusive economic rights to develop the sea floor resources, to do research, and has jurisdiction over the fisheries.   The extended continental shelf which continues beyond the 200 marine miles from the territorial sea, is an area where a country has priority rights; it has to be connected geologically and morphologically to the mainland.   The territorial sea and EEZ constitute the territory under the country's jurisdiction.

The territory under Japanese jurisdiction amounts to 4.47 mil. km^2, ranking 6th in the world in terms of area (and 4th in terms of volume (Ref. 8)).   Tokyo Metropolis manages 45% of the sea area under Japanese jurisdiction, of which Ogasawara Village owns 31%; so as a matter of fact, Tokyo could rank among the sea powers of the world.

The "sleeping" underground resources at the bottom of the sea   The waters under Tokyo's jurisdiction are known for the hydrothermal polymetallic ore deposits, among which zinc, silver, copper etc. and various other metals including precious ones.   It is indicated that there are other important reserves in the wide sea areas of the Izu-Ogasawara as well as the Myojin and Bayonnaise abyssal hills (Ref. 8).   In 2017, Japan was the first country to experimentally extract minerals from these hydrothermal polymetallic ores.

In the exclusive economic zone surrounding Minamitorishima Island, there is a high probability of finding iron, manganese, cobalt and platinum (Ref. 9).   The sea floor is also known for its rare earth deposits; this is an inclusive term for 17 elements related to the 31 known rare metals, and the sea around Japan has deposits that could last more than 200 years at the current rate of consumption. So, concerning rare earth deposits, it can be said that Japan (Tokyo) has plenty of resources for the future.

On the other hand, the sea around the Izu-Ogasawara Ocean Trench is considered for designation as a marine conservation area (Ref. 10).   A marine conservation area is designated by the country in order to protect biodiversity and the ecosystems, but such designation means limiting the economic exploitation of resources, including fisheries. While the purpose of such conservation areas is to protect and study the unique deep sea organisms, a balanced approach that also allows the exploitation of mineral resources should be considered.

Kuroshio and the fisheries   When traveling on the "Ogasawara-maru" from central Tokyo to Chichi-jima, Ogasawara (Bonin) Islands, the ship swings when crossing the Kuroshio ocean current. While the author has never experienced sea sickness, many travelers aboard seem to have a difficult time.

The Kuroshio is one of the world's powerful ocean currents, a warm one, which flows along Japan's southern coast towards north, taking an eastern direction offshore of Boso Peninsula. In the proximity of Japan, Kuroshio's width is approximately 100 km and the volume of transported water is estimated to be in the range of 20–50 million m^3/s. Compared for instance with the Amazon River which has the largest water volume in the world (approximately 200,000 m^3/s), the scale of Kuroshio is impressive. The course of Kuroshio has various segments, with areas where it follows a non-meandered channel (it flows parallel with Shikoku and the southern coast of Honshu), and areas where it has a broad-meandered channel (in the area of the Kii Peninsula and the Enshu-nada, it makes a large southward meander). When Kuroshio takes the latter broad-meandered channel, it affects the positions of fishing grounds and the fishing industry, because cold water upwells from the deep layer of the sea.

There are about 28,000 species of fish estimated in the world, out of which over 3,800 species find their habitat in the waters off the coast of Japan (Ref. 8). While Japan's calorie-based food self-sufficiency rate is approximately 40%, the rate for fish calorie is 60% (Ref. 11). Tokyo's fishing industry is the main economic sector for the island territories (Izu Oshima, Hachijojima, Ogasawara etc.). Besides the fresh fish, the industry includes processing of some special products such as *kusaya* dry fish. Due to the limitations of the freezing technology, not all of the fish caught at sea is sent to markets, but most of it is abandoned at sea. Some of the species caught are very expensive, so that thanks to the progress of transportation and preservation technology, it is expected that these problems will be solved in the future.

Another feature of the course of Kuroshio is that it has an influence on Tokyo's climate, as it was seen in Chapter 2 (see Close-up: Snow in Tokyo).

(Hiroshi Matsuyama)

Water buses on Sumida River

●**History of water buses in Tokyo and their routes**   The first water bus service to regularly operate in Tokyo was the one linking Asakusa and Ryogoku, which started in 1885 (Ref. 1).   Later on the route was extended to Eitai Bridge, and since it only costed 1 sen, it was known by the moniker "1 sen steam boat".   At the time, the bridges along the Sumida River were few, and land transportation was still underdeveloped, so the boat routes linking the eastern and western banks had to follow a zig-zag pattern.   After the chaos during and following World War II, Tokyo's water buses were revived in 1950 but during the period of high economic growth the landscape along the Sumida River's banks changed drastically with the construction of concrete embankments and highways.   Furthermore, due to water pollution, the number of passengers declined, so that in the 1960s the service stagnated.

In the mid-1970s the Sumida River's water quality improved and as a result the number of passengers recovered (Ref. 1).   In these circumstances, new public and private operators offering water bus services emerged. In 1997 alone, Tokyo Tourism Boats, Koto Ward Water Bus, Tokyo Water Line, Saitama Prefecture Arakawa Water Bus, Tokyo Ship Service, 5 new such operators offered their water bus services (Ref. 2).   The routes in 1997 mainly covered the traditional ones offered after the end of World War II but offered some additional routes towards the sea, in the area of Odaiba, the Ara and Kyu Edo Rivers, so that broader areas were being serviced.   In 2003 there were further changes, with the service on the Ara and Kyu Edo Rivers expanding routes and Koto Ward routes being discontinued.   In 2011, the water bus services were offered by only two operators, the Tokyo Tourism Boat and Tokyo Water line, and the routes were limited to the Sumida River and Odaiba.

●**Changes of routes and passenger numbers**   In terms of number of passengers by route in 1996, the highest number is that for Sumidagawa Line, followed by the Odaiba Line.   Fig. 1 shows the number of passengers on Tokyo Water Line (by river bus stop they used), based on the Report of the Association of Tokyo Parks.   According to this, most Tokyo Water Line passengers concentrate in 2 locations, the seaside located Kasai Rinkai Park and Ryogoku along the Sumida River (Fig. 1a) At other stops such as Azusawa, Kamiya, Arakawa Amusement Park, north of Sakura Bridge /Asakusa, arrivals also totaled about 4,000 passengers for each (Fig. 1a).   In 2003, the number of passengers for the above mentioned stops declines (Fig. 1a).   On the other hand, the number of passenger arrivals at Hama-rikyu Garden and Odaiba Kaihin Park, in the coastal area, witnesses an increase (Fig. 1b). According to the data, the annual number of passengers for each of Ryogoku and Odaiba Kaihin Park increases to approximately 60,000, and 50,000, respectively.   This shows that between 1997 and 2003, due to the reduction in number of routes and distances, and the evolution of number of passengers, the water bus services in Tokyo tend to concentrate along the Sumida River.

●**Water buses: from river transportation to tourist attraction**   While in the past only wider rivers such as the Sumida and Ara used to be navigable by the large scale water buses, with the introduction in 2011 by the Tokyo Water Line company of a smaller water bus "Kawasemi" it became possible to navigate the smaller rivers such as the Kanda River and Nihonbashi River, leading to the diversification of boat operations. As a result, it has become possible to admire the bridges across smaller rivers such as the Nihonbashi River or Kanda River from the water. Furthermore, since the 2000s the boats have been redesigned. Tokyo Tourist Boats implemented the design of *manga* artist Matsumoto Reiji for "Himiko" and "Hotaruna" which started operating in 2004 and, 2011, respectively (Fig. 2). **(Kei Ota)**

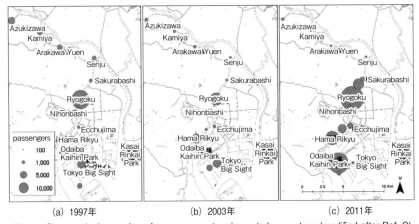

<table>
<tr><td>(a) 1997年</td><td>(b) 2003年</td><td>(c) 2011年</td></tr>
</table>

Fig. 1 Changes in the number of passengers at major waterbuses stops (modified after Ref. 2)

Fig. 2 "Himiko" waterbus designed by Matsumoto Reiji (photo by Kei Ota in February, 2012)

Natural springs and *tōfu* production

●**What are natural springs?**   Natural springs occur when groundwater naturally springs to the surface.   In recent years, under the influence of urbanization, the number of such natural springs declined, but there are actions to preserve and revive their use in some of the areas famous for such springs.   In the Metropolis, most of the natural springs can be found at shrines, temples or in parks, and those with a very good water quality are sometimes used in the production of food.   Here, we introduce the example of *tōfu* production based on good quality springs and groundwater in Tokyo.

●**Natural springs in Tokyo**   From the characteristics of landforms in Tokyo, it can be said that springs are widespread, with more than 600 natural springs currently known.   Fig. 1 shows the distribution of natural springs in the Musashino Uplands in Tokyo (Ref. 1).   The geology of the uplands includes deposits of volcanic ash—the Kanto Loam Layer, underneath which the aquifer can be found.   The Musashino Uplands consist of a succession of terraces, separated by steep cliff lines; it is at the basis of these cliff lines, in the valleys eroded by rivers, that groundwater springs.   Such spring water has been used, along with groundwater, for domestic and farming purposes since old times.

Tokyo has plentiful of spring waters, and one of the richest concentration is in the area of the Kokubunji Cliff Line.   Kokubunji Cliff Line delimitates two terraces, the Musashino Terrace and Tachikawa Terrace, running approximately 30 km parallel with the Nogawa River, along which many natural springs can be observed.   The eastern edge of the Musashino Uplands was modelled by river erosion and many narrow valleys were thus created, such indentations dividing it into narrow uplands.   As a result, natural springs occur even in some areas of central Tokyo.

●**The use of spring water and groundwater for *tōfu* production**   In areas with good quality spring/groundwater, there is a concentration of food processing businesses, using the mentioned water.   Nowadays, with stricter water sanitation standards, the use of spring groundwater for food processing is declining, but in the past sake makers, ice makers, fishmongers, businesses based on good quality water would use spring groundwater instead of tap water.

Tōfu producers also used to rely on such water.   In the production of *tōfu*, beans, water and coagulant agent (*nigari*) are essential.   In the production process based on groundwater, it is difficult to control the quality of the product, and it is believed that the final taste depends on the beans and the *nigari* agent (Ref. 2).   But with a content of water over 80%, the water plays a vital role in the production process.   The temperature of the groundwater changes little over the year, and compared with tap water the content in minerals is higher.   This is why in the past, *tōfu* producers chose to use spring/groundwater for tasty *tōfu*.

Currently, *tōfu* produced with spring water is rare and becoming a delicacy.   In Tokyo there might have been such producers in the past, but at present none is left.   However, *tōfu* made with groundwater from wells is still produced by one shop in Negishi in Taito Ward.   This is the "*Sasa no Yuki*" restaurant, which has a tradition of more than 300 years, since Edo period. The restaurant is located near the eastern edge of the Musashino Upland's cliff line and uses groundwater from a depth of 80 m for the production of *tōfu*. The poet Masaoka Shiki loved this restaurant, and he wrote many poems about it, such as "The rainy moon, cool snow in the bamboo of Negishi". The production process is unchanged ever since, so one can enjoy the original taste even now.

Some other areas, including Azabu Juban, Akasaka, Tameike etc. were also known for the quality of their water and the concentration of *tōfu* restaurants, fishmongers and Japanese restaurants. Nowadays, with spring/groundwater no longer used in food production, such concentrations of businesses are disappearing.

●**Conservation of natural springs**   In this section we have been explaining about the use of natural spring water and groundwater in the production of *tōfu* in Tokyo. The number of such natural springs is diminishing all over the country, but in Tokyo such areas could provide much-needed relief from the stress of urban life, so it is in the interest of urban residents that such places should be conserved.   (Kazuki Ishikawa)

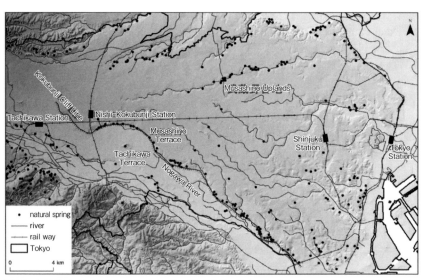

Fig. 1   Location of natural springs in the Musashino Uplands (Locations of natural springs are based on Ref. 1 (modified))

Edo's waterworks

●Shinjuku's vast water purification plant

West of Shinjuku Station, a vast water purification plant used to be located in the area where nowadays skyscrapers stand tall. From this plant, water used to be pumped all over the central area of Tokyo, but the question remains: why was this water purification plant located here? The answer can be found about 40 km west of Shinjuku, at Hamura.

●Drawing water for Edo from Tama river

Walking west from Hamura Station, we come upon the Tama River. Actually, first we come upon a channel, about 20 m wide and with a remarkable water flow (Fig. 1). This channel draws water from the nearby Tama River, and the water is transported gravitationally to central Tokyo approximately 40 km away, using the 100 m elevation gradient. In the past, this channel used to flow down to Yotsuya Okido, which was located at Naito Shinjuku (eastern side of present day Shinjuku Gyoen National Garden), but currently it becomes an underground drain east of Takaido. This is the Tamagawa Josui Waterworks.

After Tokugawa Ieyasu put the basis of Edo shogunate (feudal shogun system), the population of Edo increased rapidly. Demand for water also increased proportionally. The eastern boundary of Edo along the Sumida River (which at the time was named "Okawa") was lowland, but the western boundary was marked by the edge of the Musashino Uplands, which means higher land. These uplands were watered by smaller rivers (Shakujii, Myoshoji, Meguro Rivers etc.), but these were too distant from Edo and had not enough water. Furthermore, the uplands are covered with a thick layer of volcanic ash from Mt. Fuji and Hakone eruptions (the Kanto Loam Layer), underneath that there is the layer of terrace gravel which actually constitutes the aquifer layer here (the layer which contains the groundwater), so that in order to reach the groundwater, very deep wells would have been necessary. This is why securing water for domestic consumption was a big concern in Edo. In order to provide water to Edo's increasing population, the shogun's government started to build water supply infrastructure.

●Edo's waterworks

The government ordered the Tamagawa brothers to build waterworks system from Hamura to Yotsuya. The challenges encountered in digging the channel have been multiple, the Musashino Uplands being an area with good water permeability (therefore not quite suitable for a water channel), distant from the city and with a reduced elevation gradient between the two ends of the channel, but working with dedication, the two brothers managed to finish the project in just 7 months. The project of the Tamagawa Josui Waterworks was completed in November, 1653, approximately 50 years after the establishment of the Edo shogunate. It was an open channel from the Hamura weir to Yotsuya Okido, from where it went underground, distributing water by wooden pipes to different locations in the city of Edo. Along the wooden pipes there were wells where people could draw water for domestic uses. In some historical plays there are scenes of people congregating around the well—these are not natural wells, drawing groundwater, but wells where water was provided by the wooden pipes from the waterworks.

Edo's population kept growing to over 1 million people, making it the world's largest metropolis at the time. Edo's waterworks system was probably the largest in the world.

The Tamagawa Josui Waterworks mainly provided water to the southern areas of the city, but there were others, such as the Kanda, Sengawa, Mita, Aoyama, Kameari Josui waterworks, which together with Tamagawa Josui waterworks were called "Edo's 6 Josui waterworks". Among these, the Sengawa, Mita and Aoyama Josui waterworks derived water from the Tamagawa Josui waterworks, so it can be said that water drawn from the Tama River supplied the needs of approximately half of Edo.

●**Another role of the Tamagawa Josui Waterworks** Besides Sengawa, Mita and Aoyama waterworks, there are some 30 other such minor waterworks relying on water from the Tamagawa Josui waterworks

(Ref. 1). One of these is the Nobidome irrigation system, which is derived from the Tamagawa Josui waterworks at Kodaira observation point and flows towards Saitama Prefecture, to Niiza and Shiki Cities. This channel provides water not for domestic consumption, but for agricultural use, and was built in the attempt of transforming the Musashino Uplands into a productive farming area. The channel is quite narrow and the quantity of water flowing through it is extremely limited, but the water infiltrating from the channel helps replenish the humidity content of the soil, thus playing a very important role.

In 1893 in order to purify the water of the Tamagawa Josui Waterworks, the Yodobashi water purification plant was built in West Shinjuku, and this station functioned until 1965. For almost 300 years, the Tamagawa Josui Waterworks has continued to provide water to Edo and Tokyo.

(Daichi Nakayama)

Fig. 1 Tamagawa Josui Waterworks seen from the Hamura intake weir (photo by Daichi Nakayama in February 2011)

Tokyo's hot springs

●**What are hot springs? What are mineral springs?** The definition of hot springs is "hot water springing from the Earth, mineral water and vapor including various gases (except for those including natural hydrocarbons) that at the point of capture have a temperature above 25℃ or a content of a defined quantity of mineral components per 1 kg"(Ref. 1). Regarding the content of "mineral components" as regulated by the Hot Springs Law, there is a classification of hot springs according to temperature, pH (acid, neutral, alkali) and osmotic pressure (quantity of dissolved matter and freezing point).

Japanese hot springs, including those in Tokyo can be found in "Distribution map and catalogue of hot and mineral springs in Japan" (Ref. 2). The definition of mineral waters used in this section is "warm waters or mineral waters naturally springing from the Earth which include a high quantity of solid substances, gases or other special substances, or have a water temperature at the source well above the average air temperature of their surroundings". This means that the category of mineral waters has a wider meaning including hot springs, and is different from that of pure water (tap water that meets the standards of water quality). In the following section, we use the term "hot springs" for both the hot springs proper and mineral waters.

●**Tokyo's "hot springs": Comparing the situation in 1992 to 2018** In "Distribution map and catalogue of hot and mineral springs in Japan" (Ref. 2), an attached map shows the distribution of hot springs by administrative unit in Japan. According to this document, there were 52 hot springs in Tokyo Metropolis in 1992. In detail, there were 33 hot springs located in 17 administrative units on the mainland, and 19 located in 6 administrative units on the islands. A special notice: the 5 hot springs in Ogasawara Village are all located on Iwo-to Island, where the access of visitors is forbidden. The volcanic origin of many of these islands explains the widespread presence of hot springs. On the mainland, however, such a high number of hot springs is surprising. For example, in 1992, Ota Ward in Tokyo had 10 such hot springs, the highest number in the Metropolis.

"Distribution map and catalogue of hot and mineral springs in Japan"(Ref. 2) mentioned above was issued more than 25 years ago, so we decided to check the newest available data (September 2018) regarding Tokyo's hot springs. Since such data are not regularly published, we requested the data from the Environmental Bureau, Tokyo Metropolitan Government, and they kindly provided a list of the Metropolis' natural springs. According to the data, currently there are 175 hot springs in Tokyo (Fig. 1), distributed as follows: 133 in 43 administrative units on mainland and 42 in towns and villages on the islands. It might be a result of the recent interest in hot springs, but compared with 1992, both the number of administrative units and of hot springs has greatly increased. Again, the highest number of hot springs can be found in Ota Ward, similar with 1992, but with 23 new additions to the list. The only administrative unit where the number of hot springs declined is Ogasawara Village (from 5 to 2), and all of them on

Iwo-to Island. Fig. 1 shows the distribution of hot springs in the Metropolis. Surprisingly, of the 23 wards, only Kita Ward does not have any hot springs, while in the adjacent administrative units, only 8 do not have hot springs. Preparing this map, the author realized that Tokyo can be considered a hot spring paradise.

●**The black hot springs in and around Ota Ward**   Black hot springs can be found in Tokyo (Ref. 3); their water color is similar to Coca Cola, or to liquid ink and most of them can be found in Ota Ward's coastal areas, but also around Ueno, Asakusa, Azabu, Edogawa etc. Such black water is also used for hot spring baths.   In the Kanto Plain, black hot springs originate in comparatively deep geological layers (500 m depth), and are widespread in the metropolis.   In the coastal area, they are well known since before World War II, as they were easily discovered when digging wells to pump water in this area where groundwater is not deep and easy to dig.

The water is dark-colored from the plants that drowned in the water in geological times, from a few hundred thousand to tens of thousands of years ago.   They were decomposed in an environment deprived of oxygen, resulting in the accumulation of substances rich in carbon.   While the water looks very peculiar, it does not have a specific smell.   It contains a high quantity of sodium hydrogen carbonate and it is recognized for its beautifying properties, helping in the defoliation of old skin.

As a general trend, however, the number of hot spring baths has been declining in the Metropolis.   This is due to the penury of inheritors of hot spring bath businesses or to the aging of the equipment/infrastructure. In the 10 year interval prior to 2017, the number declined to approximately 60% (Ref. 4). In order to preserve these places for social interaction and as symbols of Japanese culture, Tokyo Metropolitan Government is implementing seminars designed to train potential managers of hot spring facilities.

(Hiroshi Matsuyama)

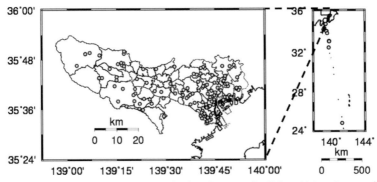

Fig. 1   Locations of hot springs and mineral waters in Tokyo Metropolis as of September 2018 (Locations of natural springs, based on the inquiry to Bureau of Environment, Tokyo Metropolitan Government).

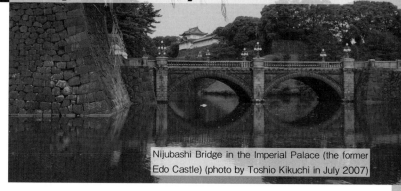

Tokyo's History and Culture

Through the creation of various urban infrastructures, Edo grew into a mega city in the 18th century. New urban development and popular culture started to flourish in the process of post-disaster recovery. Tokyo inherited the best characteristics of conventional urban development and popular culture of Edo and continues to grow as a global metropolis.

5.1 Edo Castle, the origins of Tokyo

The city of Edo   Construction of Ota Dokan's (a *samurai* warlord) castle looking over the Hibiya Inlet is generally regarded as the beginning of Edo's history. However, the history of Edo's urban development began with the construction of the great Edo Castle by Tokugawa Ieyasu, the powerful military governor (*shogun*) of the time. Tokugawa Ieyasu made various plans and

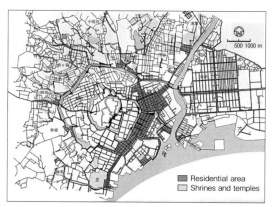

Fig. 5.1   Edo city map and land use during the Kan'ei era (1630s) (modified after Ref. 1)

unleashed ingenuity to transform Edo into a huge urban space. The completed city map of Edo in Fig. 5.1 shows the characteristics of the Kan'ei era (1630s). The Kan'ei era began before the Great Fire of Meireki (1657), and it was the time when Edo's presence as a city was prominent with and the expansion of the city boundaries. According to the city map, the spatial composition of Edo city is very different from the time when Ieyasu started to reside in the castle. One main difference was that the Hibiya Inlet, which was just east of Edo Castle, was reclaimed to create a built-up area. The other main change was the diversion of rivers including the construction of a new moat, and artificial canals, creating an urban space that spans waterways. These two projects were inter-connected. The reclamation of the Hibiya Inlet required the diversion of the river (Hirakawa) that flows into the inlet. A new canal was built connecting the east and west sides to effectively conduct the conveyance of materials by water for the development of Edo Castle. The remaining soil generated by the river diversion and the construction of the canal was used for the reclamation of the Hibiya Inlet.

Urban space that could accommodate a large population was newly secured by land reclamation on the coast. At the same time, the moats and waterways that stretch around the urban space not only functioned as a canal for water transportation of people and goods, but also as a drainage channel that removed excess water generated in the wetlands of the reclaimed area. In Edo, the land base was intentionally inclined to secure effective drainage and supply of water to support the lives of urban residents. Accordingly, Edo developed into a mega city with over 1 million people in the 18th century through various urban infrastructure developments that were carried out from the early to mid-Edo period (Ref. 2).

Urban segregation The urban space of Edo was enforced through various mechanisms. It is widely known Tenkai, that a leading Buddhist monk who served as an advisor to Tokugawa shogunate established Kan'ei-ji temple on the nothern direction (considered as *kimon* or devil's gate) and Zojo-ji temple (Ref. 3) on the southeast direction (considered as *uramon* or devil's postern) of Edo Castle in order to avoid misfortune and bad spirits enterning the castle. However, the most important mechanism in setting up an urban space in Edo was the segregation of space by occupation and social status. As is clear from the map of mid-Edo period (Fig. 5.1), the city space was broadly divided into *samurai* residential area, townsmen residential area, and religious lands such as temples and shrines accordingly.

The *samurai* residential area was arranged in a spiral shape surrounding the Edo Castle and it was mainly located on uplands or highlands. In the *samurai* residential area, there were upper, middle and lower class residencies. The level of the residence was determined with the distance to the castle and the upper level residencies where feudal lord families resided were located next to the castle. On the other hand, the townsmen residential area was located in lowland areas such as Nihonbashi in the east side of the Edo Castle, and in the valleys that carved the uplands. The cutout drawing created during the Edo period helps to distinguish between the *samurai* and townsmen residential areas, and you can roughly estimate the topography from the distribution of different land types. The religious lands spread around the periphery of the Edo region, and served as a base to protect the Edo Castle. After the mid-Edo period, the protective function of temples and shrines declined, and they tended to function as leisure spaces such as pilgrimage and tour sites (Ref. 4). For example, tours such as the "Seven Lucky Gods Pilgrimage" have been developed at temples and shrines as pilgrimage to pray for good fortune.

5.2 Edo's popular culture

"Seven Lucky Gods Pilgrimage" as popular culture   The belief in the "Seven Lucky Gods" (*shichifukujin* in Japanese) is thought to have originated among the commoners in Kyoto and it came into the limelight as the "Seven Lucky Gods Pilgrimage" during the Edo period. In response to the recommendation of the Buddhist priest, Tenkai Tokugawa Shogunate established shrines and temples that enshrine the Seven Gods of Fortune in Edo city, and encouraged the belief of "Seven Lucky Gods". The "Seven Lucky Gods Pilgrimage" began during the mid-Edo period. When people worshiped these seven deities on New Year's Day, it was believed that they could avoid seven misfortunes and enjoy seven fortunes ultimately. The "Seven Lucky Gods" started to appear on *ukiyo-e*, a Japanese art form that became popular in Edo period and the belief in "Seven Lucky Gods" became stronger among Edo people. The stable economic and social conditions that enabled people to easily demand for wealth and leisure can be seen as the reason behind the widespread popularity of the belief in "Seven Gods of Fortune" and "Seven Lucky Gods Pilgrimage".

The pilgrimage currently takes place at 43 location in Tokyo and one third of

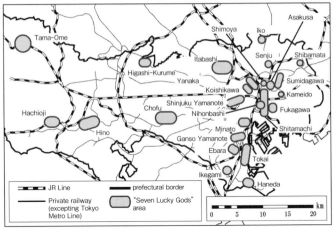

Fig. 5.2 Distribution of the "Seven Lucky Gods Pilgrimage" sites in Tokyo (based on Ref. 5)

the tours have been continuing up through today since the Edo period such as the "Seven Lucky Gods Pilgrimages" in Yanaka, the Sumida River and Fukagawa area. According to Fig. 5.2, traditional "Seven Lucky Gods Pilgrimage" is widely located in downtown areas and residential areas of ordinary people or original commercial districts and countryside, which suggest that the pilgrimage is not only a religious culture, but also a recreational (tourist) culture of the common people.

Yanaka Seven Lucky Gods Pilgrimage Yanaka Seven Lucky Gods Pilgrimage, which was established from 1751 to 1764, (during the Horeki era) is the oldest tour of this kind in Edo's history. Yanaka's course includes the Shinobazu-no-ike Benten-do temple (for *Benzaiten*, the Goddess of arts and knowledge), Gokoku-ji temple (for *Daikokuten*, the God of prosperity), Choan-ji temple (for *Jurojin*, the God of wisdom and longevity), Tenno-ji temple (for *Bishamonten*, the God of victory and dignity), Shusho-in temple (for *Hotei*, the god of fortune, guardian of children), Seiun-ji temple (for *Ebisu*, the God of business success) and Togaku-ji temple in Tabata (for *Fukurokuju*, the God of longevity and happiness, Fig. 5.3) over 5 km route. The main feature

Fig. 5.3 Togaku-ji temple with *Fukurokuju* (one of the Seven Lucky Gods) in Tabata (photo by Toshio Kikuchi in March 2006)

of the course is that it covers only temples (many "Seven Lucky Gods Pilgrimage" tours usually include shrines). Yanaka was developed as a temple town (*monzen-machi* in Japanese) around Kan'ei-ji temple in Ueno. Consequently, a religious culture flourished in the area. However, Yanaka was not simply a space of religious faith, but also a recreational site for pilgrimage tours.

Another characteristic of Yanaka's "Seven Lucky Gods Pilgrimage" is the geographical environment of the course. Yanaka was a rural village located just outside of Edo city, and was one of the day-trip destinations on the outskirts of Edo. In particular, "Higurashi-no-sato" (the origin of current Nippori) in Yanaka was well known as a good spot to enjoy seasonal flowers. When the society was stable and people could afford leisure, Higurashi-no-sato became a popular holiday destination. In this way, people enjoyed their free time by strolling around the "Higurashi-no-sato", and when the flowering season was over, "Seven Lucky Gods Pilgrimage" was held as a casual holiday activity. The attractiveness of Yanaka as a day trip destination was not only the suburban landscape and religious spaces, but also the contrast between the natural environment such as uplands and valleys. Temples were mainly located on the uplands, while villages and rice fields were located in the valleys. Yanaka's pilgrimage course, which goes down the valleys and up the uplands, provided an opportunity for people to enjoy seasonal changes in various landscapes. From the uplands, visitors could see the villages and central Edo city and also Mt. Fuji in the distance. Yanaka developed as a holiday destination by embracing and promoting the local natural landscape and culture (Ref. 6).

5.3 Western-style town planning and birth of modern Tokyo

Urban space modernization When the emperor Meiji moved his residence from Kyoto to Edo in 1868, an imperial edict was issued to rename Edo as Tokyo and the new name means "the eastern capital".

Tokyo's physical and spatial urban space went through major changes since the Meiji era. In other words, Tokyo took the first steps to become a global city by actively incorporating Western architecture and technological innovation into the urban landscape and infrastructure. Brick constructions in Ginza are an exquisite example of space modernization using Western architecture, which also contributed to the creation of a fire-resistant city, a long-cherished wish since the Edo period. Another example of modernization was the establishment of rail transportation in Tokyo (Ref. 7).

Expansion of Tokyo's urban space   Steam locomotive railways were constructed as a means of transportation between cities. Japan's first railway was opened between Shimbashi and Yokohama in 1872. Then the railways between Shimbashi and Kobe (current Tokaido Main Line), Ueno and Takasaki (current Takasaki Line), Akabane and Shinagawa were laid. The Kobu Railway (current Chuo Main Line) connecting Shinjuku and Tachikawa was opened in 1889. It was extended to Iidamachi, the city central area, and then up to Manseibashi Station. Tokyo's railways currently provide access to the north from Ueno Station, west from Manseibashi Station, and south from Shimbashi Station. At the same time, the current Joban Line and Sobu Line railways were also constructed to operate from Kitasenju and Ryogoku Stations (Fig. 5.4). These two railway stations did not give access to the city center. Therefore, streetcars were the main mode of transit at major locations in the city. The area of Tokyo city covered Tokyo's 15 wards, and it was almost in line with the Edo's city area. The operation of railways from central Tokyo to the suburbs triggered a rapid expansion of Tokyo's urban space.

Tokyo Station was completed in 1914 as the central railway station in Japan while Tojo, Keio, Tamagawa, Tobu, Keisei and Keihin Railways were laid towards the suburbs. The suburban bound railways led to the expansion of Tokyo's urban space and creation of modern Western-style cities spreading a new lifestyle to the suburbs. Tokyo's urban space expanded beyond the scope of Tokyo's 15 wards by 1914. At the same time, the range of commuting to the city center within one hour also expanded as a result of railway development.

As the number of commuters from the suburbs and residents in the suburbs increased, the population of Tokyo started to increase dramatically. A new lifestyle has spread from Tokyo to the surrounding area as a modern urban culture and many suburban residents adopted Western-style clothing, food and housing accordingly (Ref. 9).

Fig. 5.4 Railway route map in Tokyo in 1914 (modified after Ref. 8)

5.4 Disaster recovery and changes in Tokyo

Multiple disasters that hit Edo/Tokyo Edo/Tokyo has experienced major disasters multiple times. Each time, not only has the urban space been reconstructed, it has been also greatly transformed. For example, the Edo fire in 1657 broke out from Hongo Maruyama Town and burned most of the city including the core building of the Edo Castle. This great fire triggered a major remodeling of the Edo city space. The temples located in the center of Edo were moved to the outskirts of the city (for example, Kichijo-ji temple moved from Surugadai to Komagome), and the red-light district in Ningyocho (an entertainment center) also moved out of the city to Shin-yoshiwara. Broad boulevards (*hirokoji*) were constructed everywhere in the city as firebreaks, creating a fire resistant city. The current Ueno-hirokoji is known as a remnant of such a fire barrier. Even after that, Edo city was hit by several disasters such as fires, earthquakes, and the Hoei eruption of Mt. Fuji. Even in the Taisho era, the devastating Great Kanto Earthquake damaged the city, and in World War II it turned into a scorched space by air raids. However, Tokyo, like Edo, revived each time with a great transformation of urban space (Ref. 7).

City Transfiguration after the Great Kanto Earthquake A major earthquake with an epicenter beneath the floor of Sagami Bay occurred at eleven fifty-eight a.m. on September 1, 1923, causing catastrophic damage to the entire Kanto region and parts of Shizuoka and Yamanashi Prefectures. In particular, fires following the earthquake caused significant damage in the old city area of Tokyo. Fig. 5.5 shows the level of damage by the Great Kanto Earthquake.

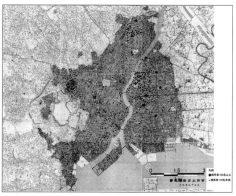

Fig. 5.5 Damage from the Great Kanto Earthquake in Tokyo (Ref.9)

Fires occurred at several places during the lunch time, and got widely spread by strong winds burning down many buildings in areas such as Nihonbashi, Kyobashi, Shitaya, Asakusa, Honjo, Fukagawa and Kanda. About 60% of houses in Tokyo were affected, and more than 60,000 people were killed or lost due to fire. Buildings such as Ryounkaku, known as the twelve stories of Asakusa, and the government offices that were the symbols of westernization collapsed, functions such as water supply, transport, broadcasting, press stopped, and the capital functions of Tokyo were completely paralyzed.

The reconstruction of Tokyo was carried out based on the "Tokyo Reconstruction Plan after the Great Kanto Earthquake" guided by Shinpei Goto, a Japanese cabinet minister. Although the city planning aspect of this revival plan has been greatly amended, it has definitely become the basis for the formation of modern urban spaces in Tokyo. The main streets of the city center and the downtown area, and a connecting community road network with a width over 4 m were developed based on the plan. In addition, land readjustment projects were carried out mainly in the areas destroyed by the earthquake, and infrastructure such as water, sewage and gas were also improved. The main streets of central city and downtown, such as Uchibori, Yasukuni, and Showa Streets, were also created under the reconstruction projects after the Great Kanto Earthquake. The bridges over the Sumida River were severely damaged by the earthquake, and the construction of permanent bridges that could withstand future earthquakes was also promoted. Nine of the current ten Sumida River bridges (except Shin-Ohashi) were reconstructed bridges (Ref. 10).

The transformation of urban space due to the Great Kanto Earthquake was not limited to the reconstruction plan. A part of people's living space and economic space was moved from the densely populated area to the suburbs to avoid damages by disasters. For example, factories that were concentrated in the downtown area near the city center were moved to Ota Ward, which was relatively less damaged by the earthquake. Ota Ward was also designated as a factory district by the City Planning Act, which has led to the development of Ota Ward's "factory town" today. On the other hand, residential areas were moved to suburbs where the damage of the earthquake was relatively low, and suburban residential areas such as Den'en-chofu and Seijo were born. In particular, the development of suburban residential areas on the Musashino Uplands was promoted in conjunction with the development of the railway network.

(Toshio Kikuchi)

Edo's spatial range

●**Vague city borders of Edo** The shogunate first marked the Edo city borders in 1698 by installing landmark poles (Ref. 1). These regulatory signs were installed at 29 locations near Asakusa, Ueno, Komagome, Koishikawa, Kohinata, Ushigome, Ichigaya, Yotsuya, Aoyama, Azabu, Shibuya and the Sumida River dividing the Edo city and its suburbs. These landmark poles helped travellers know the Edo borders. Later, in 1803, the shogunate declared the area within 16 km radius from the Edo Castle as the spatial range of Edo city. Edo tourism was flourishing and there were many travellers visiting Edo at that time. The population growth has led to many urban issues and the vague city borders of Edo also became a severe concern (Ref. 2). For example, the borders of Edo were vague when expelling criminals or suspects from Edo, and it was necessary to clarify the official borders of Edo.

●**Delineation of Edo borders based on _shubiki_ and _sumibiki_ method** In 1818, towards the end of the Edo period, the supervisor to shogunate _daimyo_ (feudal lord) Sukezaemon Makino visited both inner and outer city areas of Edo. Based on his visit, the conference chamber of Edo marked the urban area in red lines (_shubiki_) on the Edo city map and clarified the city area of Edo. At the same time, the area under the town magistrate was indicated by black lines (_sumibiki_) (Fig. 1).

The red lines basically included the lands under the jurisdiction of the magistrate of temples and shrines, and covered Sunamura, Kameido and the Naka River in the east. Yoyogi, Tsunohazu, Totsuka, Ochiai Villages and Kanda Josui waterworks in the west, Kamiosaki Village and the Meguro River in Minami-Shinagawa in the south, Senju/Oku Village, the Takino River, Itabashi, Arakawa and the Shakujii River downstream sector in the north. On the other hand, the range under the town magistrate indicated by black lines covered Nittamura, Nagasaki, Sarue Village areas in the east, Shimotakada and Okubo Villages in the west, Shimotakanawa, Nakameguro Shimomeguro in the South and Minowa, Komagome, Sugamo Villages in the north.

If you look at the old Edo map (Fig. 1), you can find an area where the red lines are pointing at the outer boundary of the city. It was where Meguro Fudo (also known as Ryusen-ji) temple was located. The temple was a popular pilgrimage site at that time. Therefore, the shogunate decided to take over the control of the area and the temple was marked as a part of the Edo city range accordingly. All the crowded places in the inner city were also included in the spatial range marked by black lines. Therefore, we can assume that the black lined areas or _sumibiki_ were mainly the leisure destinations that attracted a large crowd of people.

●**Compact Edo sightseeing** Edo city was a compact area as indicated by the landmark poles and the range of 16 km radius from Edo Castle. The city's major attractions could be explored in a day on foot.

During the late Edo period, Edo trips and attractions became popular, and the population reached nearly 1.3 million people (Ref. 3). In the social and cultural background of Tokyo, the demarcation of the urban area of Edo by red lines and the recreational area by black lines made it possible to fix a compact range for Edo sightseeing activities. However, the "old Edo red lined map" (*shubiki-zu*) does not show clear place names. The specific range of Edo can be better understood by looking at the divisional map published during the late Edo period.

●**Portable Edo *kirie-zu*** "Edo *kirie-zu*" is a large-scale old divisional map of Edo (Ref. 4) made out of picture cutouts (Fig. 2). This is an old map that has become a popular commodity of Edo, purchased by *samurai* warriors and travelers visiting Edo on job transfers or sightseeing. There were several editions of Edo *kirie-zu*. One of them, the Owariya edition (by Kirindo publishers) from 1848 to 1853 was the most popular type as a representative souvenir of Edo. The map incorporated the pictorial form of multicolored woodblock prints (Ref. 5). Owariya edition consisted of 30 maps that showed Edo regional divisions. The area drawn on the map is almost the same as the area indicated in *shubiki-zu*. While the traditional picture-cut drawings are generally drawn in four light colors, Owariya used five vivid colors and the map looked very similar to *nishiki-e* (multi-colored woodblock prints). Temples and shrines were indicated in red, forests and fields in green, rivers, ponds, and seas in blue, roads and bridges in yellow, townhouses in gray were considered as friendly and understandable drawings. By comparing the *shubiki-zu* and the Edo *kirie-zu*, we can get detailed geographical information about the Edo city area.

(Myungjiin Hong)

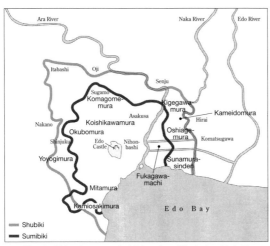

Fig. 1　Edo city area *shubiki-zu* (modified after Ref. 3)

Fig. 2　Edo *kirie-zu* of Ueno (from National Diet Library, Japan, Digital Collection)

Edo's public holidays

●**Annual events**   Various annual events were held in Edo every season. The annual events included new year celebration at the start of the year, cherry blossom viewing (*hanami*) and clamming (*shiohigari*) in spring, carp streamer (*koinobori*) festival, river fate (*kawabiraki*), Sanno festival, fireworks (*hanabi*), summer-evening festivals (*noryo*) in summer, moon rise-waiting until the twenty sixth night (*Nijurokuya-machi*), moon viewing (*tsukimi*), ginger festival (*Shoga-matsuri*) and Kanda festival in autumn, the new cast debut of the three *kabuki* theaters (*Edosanza-kaomise*), open air fair at shrines (*tori-no-ichi*), celebration of seven-three-five years of age (*shichigosan*) and year end markets (*toshi-no-ichi*) in winter (Ref. 1). As popular culture developed and spread in the early modern era, many people were able to enjoy the annual events regardless of their social status.

●**Spread of Edo *hanami* culture**   *Hanami* was one of the most popular annual holiday events in Edo. The origins of *hanami* in Edo were closely related to the construction of Kan'ei-ji temple in Ueno. When Edo became the political center that ruled Japan, the shogunate decided to build the Kan'ei-ji temple as a symbol of his authority. Also Uenoyama area was selected as the temple site where the four guardian gods were in balance (*shijin-sō*) with suitable topographic conditions and land size. *Sakura* trees were chosen as the main vegetation of the temple garden. Originally, *sakura* was not a common flower in Edo. *Sakura* trees were planted only in the gardens of private residences, temples and shrines and the number was limited to maximum of ten trees. It is well known that Tokugawa Ieyasu and

Tokugawa Hidetada were enthusiastic admirers of *sakura* blossoms. There is a written record that the advisor to the shogunate, Jigan Daishi Tenkai Buddhist monk was also a *sakura* lover and encouraged the idea of growing *sakura* trees in the proposed site of Kan'ei-ji temple (Ref. 2). In response to the desire of Tenkai monk, the third *shogun*, Tokugawa Iemitsu ordered to bring the trees from Yoshinoyama area and planted them in the temple site. In 1636, common people were also given the opportunity to view *sakura* at Kan'ei-ji temple, and a regional magazine introduced Ueno as the first *hanami* spot in Edo. Asakusa, Yanaka, Yotsuya and Shiba areas also became popular as *hanami* spots. Later, Tokugawa Yoshimune, the eighth *shogun* announced a tree-planting policy to grow *sakura* trees in Koganei area and other suburbs of Edo so that more people could enjoy the beauty of *sakura*. As a result, *hanami* rapidly spread throughout Edo. The festive atmosphere of *hanami* in the early modern times was often depicted in the scenic drawings of *ukiyo-e*. *Hanami-kosode*, a specially designed *kimono* for women is also a proof of the enormous popularity of *hanami* at that time (Fig. 1). The women went out to see *sakura* in these colorful fine clothes and enjoyed *hanami* more than any other annual event. The famous Edo *hanami* spots were created as leisure space for Edo people. Tokyo inherited the Edo *hanami* culture as a tourist attraction which continues to remain popular even today.

●**Theatres and dining out as popular forms of Edo entertainment**   There were several other forms of entertainment for people to enjoy their holidays. In particular, *kabuki* play was an entertainment that *kabuki*'s new casting in November was even announced as an annual event. *Kabuki* is derived from the *kabuki* dance performed by the shrine maiden Okuni of the Izumo Taisha shrine wearing male attire in Kyoto in 1603 (Ref. 3). Later, the shogunate banned female *kabuki* to keep the manners and customs in order and decreed a new form of *kabuki* played exclusively by male actors which was the base for today's *kabuki*. During the Genroku era, Ichikawa Danjuro, the first generation of Ichikawa family gained popularity for his rough acting stlye, and *kabuki* fully matured during the Bunka and Bunsei eras. The four theaters Yamamuraza, Nakamuraza, Murayamaza (later Ichimuraza) and Moritaza known as "Edo Shiza" were the most famous *kabuki* theaters in Edo. Some other playhouses such as Yukiza and Satsumaza in Nihonbashi, Asakusa and Ryogoku areas were also lively with many *kabuki* loving people.

According to the Edo guidebook, there were many restaurants in Edo including expensive restaurants offering high-ranked *kai-* *seki* and *kabayaki* cuisines (menus costed around 200 *mon* equivalent to 5000 yen today), as well as reasonably priced restaurants offering *soba* noodles, *sushi*, and *ochazuke* (costed less than 50 *mon*). Many restaurants were concentrated in the Nihonbashi area, the center of Edo economy, and the Asakusa area, where the oldest temple of Edo (Senso-ji) was located (Fig. 2). Edo restaurants were mainly located in and around the theaters and famous temples and shrines. Restaurants in the Asakusa area were concentrated in Monzen-cho near Raijin-mon and Ninten-mon and the distribution pattern implies that Edo people enjoyed eating out while watching a play or visiting a temple or shrine.

Edo people at that time seemed to spend their money lavishly for leisure purposes, and to relish such activities frequently. Therefore, during the Edo public holidays, people spent their time enjoying *sakura*, *kabuki* performances, eating out, on pilgrimage tours, fireworks, ceremonial exhibitions and shopping.   (Myungjin Hong)

Fig. 1   A lady wearing a *hanami-kosode* (from National Diet Library, Japan, Digital Collection, 'Toto meisho awase Ueno')

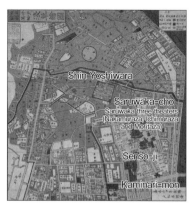

Fig. 2   Asakusa dotted with restaurants (from National Diet Library, Japan, Digital Collection, "Edo kirie-zu" 'Imado Minowa Asakusa ezu')

地理学基礎シリーズ

好評既刊をオールカラーで改訂。
【2020年2月刊行！】

地理学基礎シリーズ 3
地誌学概論【第2版】
矢ヶ崎典隆・加賀美雅弘・牛垣雄矢 編著
朝倉書店

地誌学概論【第2版】

矢ヶ崎典隆・加賀美雅弘・牛垣雄矢 編著

B5判・184頁 定価（本体 3,400 円＋税）
（16820-4）C3325

● 地域調査に基づくミクロな視点からグローバルな問題まで、気候や地形、人々の生活や文化、社会や経済の仕組みなど幅広く解説。

● 7つの地誌学的アプローチに沿って構成しており、丸暗記の地理ではなく、「地理的なものの見方」が身に付く。

● 中学・高校の社会科教師を目指す学生や、現役の社会科教員の方にもおすすめ。

2. 身近な地域の地誌
—神奈川県川崎市の地域調査—

2.1 地域学習の視点
—身近な地域の地誌の特徴を—

2.2 現代の川崎市の地誌的特徴

2.3 空間的視点から身近な地域を理解する

写真や地図を
オールカラーで！

地理学基礎シリーズ

1 地理学概論（第2版）

B5判 180頁 (16819-8)

定価（本体3,300円＋税）

中学・高校の社会科教師を目指す学生のためのスタンダードとなる地理学の教科書を改訂。現代の社会情勢、人類が直面するグローバルな課題、地球や社会に生起する諸問題を踏まえて、地理学的な視点や方法を理解できるよう、具体的に解説した。

2 自然地理学概論

高橋日出男・小泉武栄 編著

B5判 180頁 (16817-4)

定価（本体3,300円＋税）

中学・高校の社会科教師を目指す学生にとってスタンダードとなる自然地理学の教科書。自然地理学が対象とする地表面とその近傍における諸事象をとりあげ、具体的にわかりやすく、自然地理学を基礎から解説している。

■地理学基礎シリーズに続く、初級から中級向けの地理学シリーズ。

シリーズ〈地誌トピックス〉

全3巻完結・B5判 各定価（本体3,200円＋税）

1. グローバリゼーション —縮小する世界—
2. ローカリゼーション —地域へのこだわり—
3. サステイナビリティ —地球と人類の課題—

全3巻完結！

■教員を目指す学生のための日本の地誌学のテキスト。

世界地誌シリーズ

B5判・各定価（本体3,400円＋税）

1. 日本
2. 中国
3. EU
4. アメリカ
5. インド
6. ブラジル
7. 東南アジア・オセアニア
8. アフリカ
9. ロシア
10. 中部アメリカ
11. ヨーロッパ

図3 最大の旅客機をあやつる巨大スタジアムの設備を…

図2 …ロシアのツーリズム
2018年、首都南部

POCUS4 ロシアのツーリズム 149

書名　地誌学概論　[第2版]　定価（本体 3,400 円＋税）（16820-4）

価格は 2020 年 3 月現在。　ISBN は 978-4-254-16820-4 を省略

朝倉書店

〒162-8707　東京都新宿区新小川町6-29　TEL：03-3260-7631　FAX：03-3260-0180
http://www.asakura.co.jp　E-mail：eigyo@asakura.co.jp

【お申込み書】このお申込み書にご記入の上，最寄りの書店にご注文ください。

------------------------------ 【キリトリ線】 ------------------------------

書名		冊
書名		冊

お名前	ご住所	取扱書店
	TEL	

Close-up

Tokyo's place names

●Place names as a historical reflection

A place name is the official name given to a particular land. In Japan, a place name itself implies an idea of the lifestyle and natural landscape of its area. For example, place names with the *kanji* characters for a cliff, summit, and slope came from a mountain area while those with the characters for a stream, inlet, waterfall and pool originated in a riverside area. Also, place names with the *kanji* characters for a beach, sandbank, and cape were named after a coastal area. In this way, place names related to nature such as mountains, rivers, seas, forests, fields, valleys, wastelands, basins, plateaus, passes, hot springs, and springs can be identified as "nature-based place names" and place names related to human activities such as cities, religion, leaders and town planning as "culture-based place names" (Ref. 1). Place names can be further classified into "administrative place names" (for example, Akasaka 1-*chome*) designated by the government and "popular names" (for example, Yoshiwara).

●Nature-based place names

The former name of Tokyo, "Edo" literary means "the river entrance", and geographically it means the estuary at the river mouth. Ikebukuro, Ueno, Shitaya, and Yanaka in Tokyo are also nature-based place names. The name "Ikebukuro" uses the *kanji* character for "pond"(*ike*). Ikebukuro's "*bukuro*" means "reservoir" created by flooding of a large river. Therefore, when classified by landform type, the name Ikebukuro has originally derived from "river" and not from "pond" (Ref. 1). Place names with the *kanji* character for "a well" (井) such as Koganei (小金井) and Nukui (貫井) that are distributed along the

Kokubunji Cliff Line have derived from the meaning "spring water". A "valley" (谷) refers to the elongated depression between the mountains. For example, Yanaka (谷中) is located in a valley. Entering the Meiji era, the nature-based place name "Edo" was replaced with the culture-based place name "Tokyo" meaning "the eastern capital".

●Culture-based place names

Many of the culture based place names in Tokyo are associated with the Edo shogunate's town planning system. For example, the areas where officials who managed rickshaws and horses (for the purpose of communication and transport) lived were named "Kodenmacho" and "Odenmacho" with the meaning "small and big horse messenger towns". "Okachimachi" derived from the residencies of the *okachigumi*, foot guards in the Edo shogunate. The place names "Akasaka-mitsuke" and "Yotsuya-mitsuke" mean the locations of Edo Castle's security check points (*mitsuke*). The place name "Aoyama" derived from the name of a *samurai* Aoyama Tadanari whose mansion was located in the Aoyama area. "Marunouchi" with the meaning "the outer moat of the Edo Castle", "Ote-mon", "the main gate of the Edo Castle", and "Bakurocho", area where people in charge of transportation lived are some other examples of place names related to the town planning of the Edo shogunate. As mentioned above, many culture-based place names related to the historical lifestyle of Japanese people are distributed around the current Imperial Palace (Fig. 1). There are also place names related to religion. For example, "Meguro" and "Mejiro" were named after "Meguro Fudo" and "Mejiro Fudo", two of the "Five colored Fudo" (Goshiki-fudo) temples. "Higashi Ginza", "Nishi Shinjuku", and "Kita Shinjuku" are place names that have incorporated the name of a popular area as a brand name. This trend is still seen today, with many shopping streets incorporating the name "Ginza" (see Close-up: Ginza in Tokyo in Chapter 7).

●**Place name changes** Tsukishima in Chuo Ward, Tokyo is a typical example of a place name that changed from a culture-based place name to a nature-based one. Tsukishima was formed by the adjacent offshore islands of Ishikawajima and Tsukudashima, Tsukudashima Fort, and several landfills created after the Meiji era. Ishikawajima, which was called "Yoroijima" originally, was named in remembrance of Shoji Ishikawa who moved to the island in 1626 (Ref. 2). Ishikawajima during the Edo period played an important role in protecting the Edo harbor.

On the other hand, in 1644, the shogunate gave some island lands to 33 fishermen who migrated from Tsukuda village in Settsu-kuni (present day Osaka) to Edo. The migrants settled in the area, and named the island "Tsukudashima" after their previous hometown "Tsukuda". In 1864, a new landfill called Tsukudashima Fort was created to the south of Tsukudashima. This was a military base with a camp for soldiers who operated the cannons. Tsukishima was reclaimed in 1884 under the Tokyo Bay Channel Dredging Project by Tokyo Prefecture, and by 1896 Tsukishima's first stage, second stage and Shin-tsukudashima were built as newly-reclaimed lands. In 1967, Tsukuda (deriving from Tsukudashima), Tsukishima, Kachidoki, Toyomi-cho, and Harumi became the new Tsukishima area. Concisely, Tsukishima is composed of the historic Tsukuda district, and the modern Tsukishima district. Many factories have moved into the new land of Tsukishima, and the population has also increased since then. Today, Tsukishima is one of Tokyo's most famous spots with an interesting contrast of modern high-rise buildings of Tsukishima district and downtown atmosphere of little Tsukuda bridge area (Fig. 1).   (Myungjin Hong)

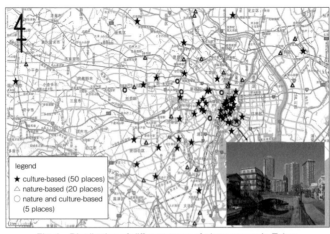

Fig. 1   Distribution of different types of place names in Tokyo

legend
★ culture-based (50 places)
△ nature-based (20 places)
○ nature and culture-based (5 places)

Edo's food culture

●The diet of Edo, dining in the Edo period   Tokyo's food has its roots in Edo's food and people continue to enjoy Edo-style cuisine in Tokyo even today.   In Edo, a majority of the common people such as laborers, craftsmen and servants were unmarried men who came to Edo for work from rural areas.   They lived in terrace houses where there were no kitchen facilities and they had to buy regular meals from somewhere, which led to the development of an inexpensive eating-out culture in Edo city (Ref. 1).   The popular food culture of Edo was passed down to Tokyo and it continued to flourish as Tokyo's food culture since then.

●*Edomae-zushi*   *Edomae-zushi* is the most known Edo-style cuisine worldwide.   It is a type of hand-formed *sushi* (*nigiri-zushi*) that combines vinegared rice with fish from Edo bay such as spotted shad, horse mackerel and sea bream.   Even though there are various opinions on its origin, it is widely accepted that Hanaya Yohei of *Yohei-zushi* in the Ryogoku area initiated the idea of *Edomae-zushi* during the Bunka-Bunsei era (1804-1830) of the late Edo period.   In the early Edo period, Kyoto–Osaka originated "*Narezushi*", (*sushi* fermented with rice and fish by lactobacillus) was the most popular kind of *sushi* and by the mid-Edo period, "*oshi-zushi*"(layers of rice, fish and other ingredients pressed in a mould) became widely popular.   Compared to these sophisticated varieties of *sushi*, *Edomae-zushi* was a very novel style based on simple hand-molding of rice and fish.

   Edomae-zushi was not only a hand-molding or *nigiri*, but its ingredients and taste were also different from the traditional kinds of *sushi*.   The soy sauce used in *Edomae-zushi* was not the traditional *kudari-shoyu* (or the light-coloured soy sauce that had been distributed to Edo from Kyoto–Osaka areas), but the rich *Jimawari-shoyu*, a local soy sauce from Shimousa province (the suburb of Edo), which had rapidly increased its market share in Edo during the Bunka-Bunsei era.   The local soy sauce had a strong flavor and aroma due to its long maturing period, and also enhanced the taste of *sushi* ingredients.   At the same time, vinegar rice was made from *kasu* vinegar from Mikawa area, present-day Aichi Prefecture, instead of traditional rice vinegar.   *Kasu* vinegar, which is brewed from *sake* lees, was popular and widely used in *sushi* restaurants in Edo as it gave moderate sweetness and sourness to rice and it was also cheaper than rice vinegar.   Even today, the custom of adding sugar to vinegar to sweeten the rice is said to be a remnant of using kasu vinegar during the Edo period.   *Edomae-zushi* with innovative ingredients and recipes was served not only at high-end restaurants such as *Yohei-zushi*, but also available at simple food stalls as an easily enjoyable eating-out.   *Edomae-zushi* was, in a manner, a variety of fast food for Edo people.

●*Soba* and *Tempura*   Similar to *Edomae-zushi*, *soba* (buckweat noodle) and *tempura* can also be pointed out as fast food dishes fostered in the city of Edo.   In the early Edo period, *soba* was not as popular as *udon* (Japanese wheat noodle) and even if *soba* was served, it was common to steam after lightly boiling the noodles, as the noodles get broken by boiling due to the lack of techniques of milling and hand-making of noodles at the time. During the Kyoho era (1716–1736), handling of *soba* became easier with the improvement of noodle making technology such as the usage of wheat flour as a thickening ingredient and development of easy to cook *soba* noodles. In addition, the thick local soy sauce was used in *soba* soup to suit the taste of Edo people and *soba* began to permeate among the common people. As a result, night *soba* stalls called "*yotaka-soba*" and "*fūrin-soba*" came to appear and gained great support from the Edo people as facilities for easy evening meals (Fig. 1). Even though night sales were banned in Edo due to the risk of fire related hazards, the *soba* night stalls were permitted tacitly to operate due to the high popularity among people.

On the other hand, *tempura* is said to have originated from *Nagasaki-tempura*, which was introduced from Portugal to Japan during the Azuchi-Momoyama era. *Nagasaki-tempura* used a thick tasted batter and the batter was also to be enjoyed along with other ingredients. This type of *tempura*

used a large amount of cooking oil, which was a high-grade ingredient at the time, making it difficult for ordinary people to reach. However, in the Edo period, the production of rapeseed cooking oil increased, and *tempura* could make its own evolution in Edo. Edo *tempura* was fried in a thin batter to bring up the full taste of Edo-style *tempura* ingredients such as conger, spotted shad and *Shiba-ebi*. The fried *tempura* was skewered and sold at street stalls. *Tempura* itself was lightly seasoned and Edo people used to dip *tempura* in their favourite thick soy sauce mixed with mirin and broth to suit their taste. *Tempura* was popular among ordinary people as a handy snack as *tempura* sold at food stalls was cheap, about four mon (corresponding to 20 to 30 yen in present currency value) per skewer, and it was also an energy source for people to intake fat.

● **From Edo to Tokyo's food culture**

When Edo changed to Tokyo in the Meiji era, western-style dishes called *Yōshoku* such as *gyūnabe* (or beef hotpot, the origins of *sukiyaki*), *tonkatsu* (or pork cutlet), *korokke* (or croquette), and *karēraisu* (or curry and rice), emerged. During the Taisho and Showa eras, westernization of the food itself progressed, making it difficult to sustain the unique food culture of Edo. Even in such circumstances, people continued to love *Edomae-zushi*, *soba*, and *tempura*, and a wide range of them from high-grade and reasonable dishes exists even today, implying that Tokyo's food culture is rooted in Edo's food culture. (Ryo Iizuka)

Fig. 1 A *soba* stall ("Nihachi-soba Yohei" by Utagawa Toyokuni III)

Chapter 6

Living in Tokyo

High-rise apartments and Chuo-Ōhashi Bridge in Tsukishima

Tokyo's population (including the neighboring prefectures) is more than one-quarter of Japan's population, and continues to grow even though Japan's overall population is in rapid decline. This chapter reveals the population structure and housing of people living in Tokyo utilizing the maps of demographic data.

6.1 Tokyoites

Tokyo's increasing population   There are 13.51 million people in Tokyo as of 2015.   The total population Tokyo and of the three neighboring prefectures reached 36.13 million, and one in four people in Japan live in the Tokyo metropolitan area.

The population of Tokyo started to increase since the period of high economic growth that began in the 1950s and stopped growing in 1960s.   The population of Tokyo metropolitan area including the three neighboring prefectures still continued to increase, and a "doughnut" phenomenon could be observed where the population in the city center was hollowed out (Fig. 6.1).   However, since

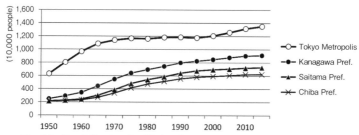

Fig. 6.1   Population trends of Tokyo (based on National Population Census)

2000, a significant population increase continues in Tokyo.

Heavy concentration of population in Tokyo   There are various reasons why people move to Tokyo.   One key reason that draws people is its high wages.   According to a prefectural survey conducted by the Ministry of Health, Labor and Welfare on the new minimum hourly wages in 2018, Tokyo ranked top (985 yen), and Kagoshima Prefecture ranked the lowest (761 yen), about 1.3 times lower compared to Tokyo (Ref. 1).

As a result of the high wages, many people are attracted to Tokyo and wish to move to Tokyo.   Capital functions and the headquarters of private companies are largely concentrated in Tokyo, and many people move to Tokyo for job transfers or seek jobs that do not exist in rural areas (see Chapter 7).

Youngsters around the age of twenty including new graduates are more likely to move to Tokyo than the older generation.   In this age group, there are a high percentage of students who move away from their parents when they enter university or find employment.   About 750,000 people, or 26.1% of all university and graduate students in Japan are concentrated in the Tokyo Metropolis (Ref. 2), which inevitably attracts young people.   At the same time, there are many people who are moving in search of a free way of living in the large metropolis with a great level of social anonymity, which in return accelerate the population concentration in Tokyo.

6.2　Urban expansion and formation of residential suburbs

Railway-led suburbanization   As the population increases, a shortage of housing in the built-up areas occurs.   Consequently, new residential areas are rapidly developed in the suburbs.   The full-scale suburbanization in Tokyo began after the Great Kanto Earthquake in 1923.   The damage caused by the earthquake was large in the densely populated lowland areas extending eastward from the city center.   Therefore, the urban area expanded to the western upland, where the damage was low (see Close-up: Tokyo's historic Shitamachi and Yamanote).   The reason behind the urban expansion was the development of a railway network that carried people from the suburbs to the city center for commuting and shopping.

At the beginning of the Showa era, railways extending from the main stations along the Yamanote Line such as Shinjuku, Shibuya, and Ikebukuro to the suburbs opened, and residential development along the railway-related real

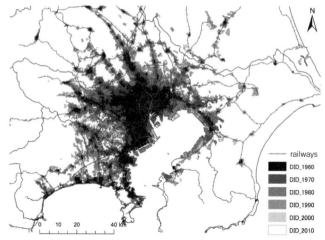

Fig. 6.2 Expansion of DID in Tokyo area and railways (based on Digital National Land Numerical Information)

estate companies of Odakyu, Tokyu, and Seibu was progressing (see Chapter 5). As shown on Fig. 6.2, the distribution of the densely inhabited district (DID) in the Tokyo area has expanded along the railway since the 1970s. In particular, the urban expansion to the suburbs was conspicuous with the steep rise in land prices during the bubble economy period in the latter half of the 1980s. Even now, when a new railway station opened, the population increases and land prices rise in the area surrounding the new railway station.

New Town Development   During the period of high economic growth after World War II, Tokyo received a large in flow of population from rural areas, and housing shortage became a serious concern. The Tokyo Metropolitan Government and the Japan Housing Corporation (now the Urban Renaissance Agency) promoted the development of new towns as a measure to overcome the issue (see Close-up: Revival of Tokyo's new towns). Tama New Town is the largest new town in Japan and accommodates a population of over 200,000 people. Tama New Town (Fig. 6.3), which was developed in a hilly area about 30 km away from the city center, was originally planned as a

Fig. 6.3 Residential area of Tama New Town (photo by Yoshiki Wakabayashi in November 2019)

commuter town. Therefore, the new town has few business and employment opportunities and people are compelled to commute far away for work, establishing a segregated lifestyle.

6.3 Residential mobility and tendency for living in the city

Housing conditions and Housing *Sugoroku*   In Tokyo, where the nation's highest land prices and population density are seen, residents have to live in small houses, pay high rents and land prices. According to the Housing and Land Statistics Survey in 2013, the ratio of homeowners in Tokyo was 45.8% (national average 61.7%), and the total area per home was 63.54 m^2 (national average 92.97 m^2). Although there has been some improvement compared to the past, it is still at the lowest level by prefecture. In addition, due to the high land prices, the ratio of detached houses in the residential area is only 27.8% (54.9% on average nationwide), and about 70% is shared houses (such as apartments and condominiums). As a result, households with children tend to move from confined residential areas to spacious suburbs.

"Housing *Sugoroku*" defines the residential movement in large cities during the period of high economic growth. The process of starting one's life from the hometown to living in boarding houses or rented apartments and finally having one's owned-house is expressed in the concept of Housing *Sugoroku*. The end result of the process was a detached house with a garden in the suburbs. The Japanese government has been promoting the homeownership policy in order to boost the Housing *Sugoroku*.

However, in the modern version of the Housing *Sugoroku*, both the beginning and the end are becoming diversified. For example, during the period of high economic growth when there were many local residents, the starting point was generally outside the metropolitan area. At that time, moving to one's own house was considered a step-up in life after living in rented apartments. However, now that the children have become the second generation in the suburbs, it is also possible to acquire a home by living with parents or inheriting from family. In addition, the number of double-income households has increased and the number of people who are oriented to the city center where work and residential proximity is easier than in the suburbs is increasing. As a result, an increasing number of people choose apartments in the city center as the end result of the Housing *Sugoroku*.

In particular, high-rise condominiums of 20 stories or more have increased since 2000 when deregulation policy has progressed. After a temporary decline due to the Lehman shock in 2008, the number continues to grow again. Out of the high-rise condominiums that were scheduled to be built after 2018, Tokyo has 123 buildings, accounting for 51.1% of the total nationwide.

Return to the city center phenomenon and shrinking suburbs   The difference between the bubble economy period and the subsequent population growth pattern as shown in Fig. 6.4 indicates the changes that occurred in the Housing *Sugoroku*.   Until the bubble economy period in the early 1980s, when land prices continued to soar, the number of people moving to the suburbs as the life stage progressed led to a population decline in the city center (the "doughnut" phenomenon).   However, in the latter half of the 1990s, when land prices fell, the difference in housing prices between the suburbs and the city center shrunk, and the population recovery in the city center became prominent. A remarkable population increase during this period can be seen in the areas where the redevelopment took place, particularly between the city center and the Tokyo Bay area, where large-scale condominiums were constructed.

As the population returns to the city center, the population in the suburbs decreases and the number of vacant houses increases. Fig. 6.5 shows the rate of decreasing population and increasing vacant houses by municipality.   The phenomenon is evident in the southeastern part of Chiba Prefecture, Minami Boso and northern Saitama municipalities, where there is limited accessibility to

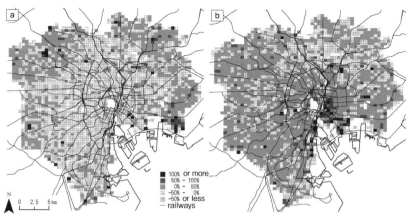

Fig. 6.4   Population changes in Tokyo wards (modified after Ref. 3)
(a) 1985-1995, (b) 1995-2005

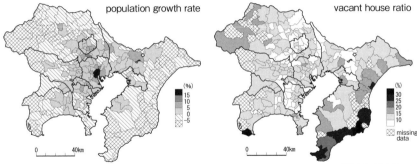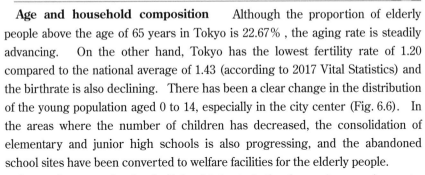

population growth rate   vacant house ratio

(%) 15 10 5 0 -5

(%) 30 25 20 15 10 ☒ missing data

0 ⊢ 40km   0 ⊢ 40km

Fig. 6.5 Population growth rate by municipality in Tokyo metropolitan area (2010-2015) and vacant house ratio in 2013 (based on National Population Census, and Housing and Land Statistics Survey)

central Tokyo. On the other hand, the vacant house rate remains low in central Tokyo, where population growth is significantly high.

6.4 Changes in population composition and distribution

Age and household composition Although the proportion of elderly people above the age of 65 years in Tokyo is 22.67% , the aging rate is steadily advancing. On the other hand, Tokyo has the lowest fertility rate of 1.20 compared to the national average of 1.43 (according to 2017 Vital Statistics) and the birthrate is also declining. There has been a clear change in the distribution of the young population aged 0 to 14, especially in the city center (Fig. 6.6). In the areas where the number of children has decreased, the consolidation of elementary and junior high schools is also progressing, and the abandoned school sites have been converted to welfare facilities for the elderly people.

One major cause for the declining birthrate is the decreasing marriage rate. The unmarried rate in the age group of 30-34 is 42.5% for men and 35.5% for women in Tokyo and tends to further increase. In addition, the scale of households is also becoming smaller, and the ratio of single households in Tokyo is 47.3% , which is the highest in the country (according to the National Population Census in 2015).

Population segregation by occupation In Tokyo, the difference in occupational composition in the western uplands and the eastern lowlands has become apparent since the beginning of modern times. White-collar job rate such as professional or technical jobs is higher in the western side compared to

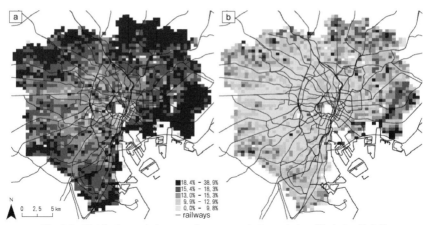

Fig. 6.6　Distribution and changes of young population ratio (modified after Ref. 3)
(a)1985, (b)2005

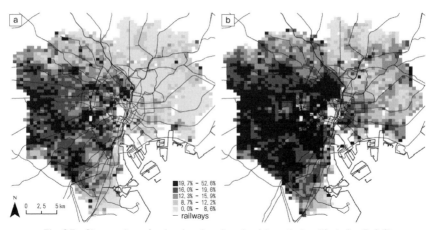

Fig. 6.7　Changes in professional and engineering jobs ratio (modified after Ref. 3)
(a)1985, (b)2005

the eastern side.　However, compared to 1985, there is a slight change in the pattern in 2005, where white-collar job rate has increased in the coastal and eastern lowlands.　This is a result of the return to the city center phenomenon (Fig. 6.7).

Foreign residents and ethnic towns　Since the bubble economy period, the number of foreigners working in Japan has increased due to the high value of the yen and revisions to the Immigration Control and Refugee Recognition Law. The number of foreign residents in Tokyo continues to increase and particularly,

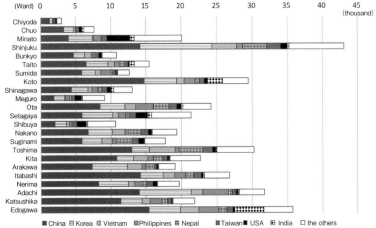

Fig. 6.8 Residential areas of foreigners by nationality (based on Basic Resident Register (January 2019))

there are a relatively large number of people from East Asia, Europe and the United States compared to other regions. If you look at Fig. 6.8, which shows the distribution of foreign residents, you can see that the distribution varies depending on their nationality.

The South and North Korean community in Tokyo is concentrated in Arakawa, Taito, and Adachi Wards. Most of them have permanent residency status in Japan as they have been residing in Tokyo for a long period, even before the World War II. There are ethnic towns in Shinjuku Ward that are emerging as urban tourist destinations. The Korea Town in Okubo district is one representative example.

Distribution of Chinese community can be mainly seen in the same areas as the Korean community. However, Chinese residential areas can also be found in Toshima and Koto Wards. Filipino population is distributed in the inner areas such as Adachi, Koto, and Ota Wards, and overlaps with the distribution of some Chinese residential areas, however, a clear settlement area could not be found. Unlike these Asian communities, Americans and other westerners are mainly gathered in Minato, Meguro and Shibuya Wards in the southern parts of Yamanote Line, where embassies, foreign-affiliated companies and foreign schools are largely concentrated.

(Yoshiki Wakabayashi)

Tokyo's historic Shitamachi and Yamanote

●**Bridges and hills** Shitamachi and Yamanote are historic names of old downtown and hillside areas of Tokyo. A widely conveyed story to taxi drivers in Tokyo asking them to "remember the names of the bridges in Shitamachi and names of the hills in Yamanote", describes the characteristics of the two areas comprehensively. However, a clear geographical definition does not exist and the two areas are generally known as the east and west or lowland and highland of Tokyo.

Tokyo, taking advantage of its topographic conditions, has flourished as a castle town centering on Edo Castle. The castle town was divided broadly into a samurai district, a temple and shrine estate and a townsmen district. The samurai district occupied more than two-thirds of the area. Particularly, the feudal lord's mansions (*daimyo-yashiki*) were built on the hillside of Yamanote surrounding the *Samurai* residencies to benefit from the favorable conditions of the location, topography and landscape. On the other hand, only about 15% of the land area was designated for townsmen, mostly in the low land areas or downtown (see Chapter 5). We can say much attention has been paid to topographic conditions and social hierarchy during the development of Edo (Ref. 1, 2). These natural and social conditions are still taken into consideration in Tokyo at varying levels.

●**Changes in administrative divisions**
The administrative divisions of Tokyo are comprised of 23 wards. Several changes took place before the establishment of the current system including the "large-small ward system" (*Daiku-shoku sei*) in November 1871, "15 wards and 6 counties system" (*Ku-gun*) in July 1878, and the "Municipal Government Act" (*Shi-cho-son sei*) in May 1889 by which Tokyo with its multiple wards was turned into a single city (Fig. 1), "Greater Tokyo" (*Dai-Tokyo*) expansion of the city from 15 wards to 35 wards in 1932 by incorporating 82 towns and villages in five outlying counties as new 20 wards (5 counties shown in Fig. 6.1), "addition of Chitose and Kinuta Villages" in 1936 (part of present Setagaya Ward), and establishment of the range equivalent to the current 23 wards of Tokyo. After a concrete reorganization in 1947 after World War II, the number of wards was officially decided to 23, resulting in the current system.

●**Population growth and urbanization**
Looking at the demographical changes, the postwar boom of the Russo-Japanese War and World War I had a notable impact on the population growth in Tokyo. As a result, agricultural areas around Tokyo were rapidly urbanized since the 1910s. However, Tokyo was hit by two major natural disasters.

The first was a typhoon and heavy rain in August 1910, which destroyed 120,000 households and killed 30 people. The second was a tsunami in October 1917, causing damage to more than 70,000 households and 699 human casualties. All the damage took place mainly in the eastern region (downtown areas) of Tokyo City, manifesting the vulnerability of lowlands to disasters.

In general, rapid urbanization leads to urban sprawl. Anticipating the forthcoming development of city centers, some suburban farmers proactively remodeled their farmlands into urban areas by utilizing the land readjustment projects. At the same time, some others attempted housing development projects focusing on promoting an ideal living environment for urban people. For example, based on the idea of "The Garden Cities of To-morrow" by an English urban planner E. Howard, Den'en Toshi Company was established in 1918 under Shibusawa Eiichi to develop a garden city offering good living environment in rapidly urbanizing Tokyo. The company started selling houses in Senzoku area in July 1922 and Tamagawadai area (present Den'en chofu) in August 1923.

●Impact of the Great Kanto Earthquake

Unfortunately, the Great Kanto Earthquake occurred on September 1, 1923, soon after the house sales. More than 100,000 people were reported to have died in the fire. In particular, the damage in the downtown area where wooden houses were densely packed was enormous. A devastating firestorm occurred at a clothing depot (present Sumida Ward) to where about 40,000 citizens had fled to take refuge during the earthquake. 38,000 of them had been burned or suffocated to death in the firestorm causing a mass loss of life. While the downtown area was severely damaged, the damage at Yamanote, the upper part of the plateau was considerably smaller. A newspaper advertisement about the Garden City published after the disaster stated, "this earthquake proved that the Garden City is a safe zone. Even the costly earthquake and fire resistant constructions cannot match the power of the natural ground and its movement. Our housing district fortunately has this blessing" (Fig. 2).

Relatively less damage in the highland areas led to the subsequent development of Yamanote suburbs. Many people moved out of Tokyo City to the suburbs including the surrounding 5 counties, and a rapid population growth occurred in the suburban areas of Tokyo. The population of Tokyo City and the surrounding 5 counties was 2.17 million and 1.18 million in 1920 and after the earthquake, respectively, the numbers increased to 2.70 million and 2.90 million respectively in 1930, reversing the relationship between Tokyo City and its suburbs (Totaled from census results). Population growth in the suburbs became prominent and resulted in an expansion of "Shitamachi" and "Yamanote" areas after the Edo period.   (Ryo Koizumi)

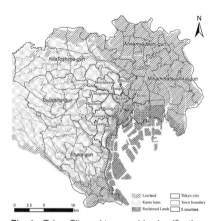

Fig. 1   Tokyo City and topographic classification

Fig. 2   Sales advertisement in 1923 (Ref. 3)

Revival of Tokyo's new towns

●**What is a "new town"?** "New town" is a newly developed urban area in the suburbs to relieve overcrowding in the city centers. As shown in Fig. 1, many new towns have been developed in the Tokyo metropolitan area since the period of high economic growth. However, most of these new towns are old now with aging populations and decaying buildings. Regeneration of the aging new towns has become a vital challenge in Tokyo. Here, we introduce the current situation of Tama New Town as a typical example of Tokyo's new towns.

●**Concept of Tama New Town** Tama New Town is located in the Tama hills about 30 km west of central Tokyo, and its area spans over four cities from Inagi to Machida Cities. Development of the new town began in 1966 by a public organization mainly under the Japan Housing Corporation (The Urban Renaissance Agency or UR at present) and Tokyo Metropolitan Government, and moving-in started in 1971 in Suwa–Nagayama in the southern part of Tama City. Even though the development of Tama New Town was officially completed in the mid 2000s, private firms are still carrying out housing development in the area. The population as of October 2019 was approximately 224,000 people.

Land use on the hills and valleys are different in the new town. Publicly funded housing complexes (*danchi*) consisting of mid-rise apartments were developed on the hilltop. Main roads and railways were constructed in the valleys, along which different types of houses, roadside commercial facilities and other buildings line up together. At the same time, "centers" with various shops

and public spaces were also created systematically. The small shopping streets in the housing complex are the immediate "centers", and the larger commercial areas around Nagayama, Tama Center and Minami-Osawa Stations are the core "Centers".

●**Aging population and associated issues** Tama New Town today is increasingly challenged with the declining and aging of its population due to the changes in household composition, especially in the early occupancy areas (Fig. 2). Most families were young and childrearing at the time they moved to the new town. However, the children are grown-ups now and have moved out of the new town to live in their preferred places and the parents who remained are aged now. Even the new occupants who move into the public housing at present are mainly composed of elderly households.

Population decline and aging are also causing a significant decline in necessary facilities for daily life. The closure of shops and medical clinics in the immediate "center" is a serious problem for people with low mobil-

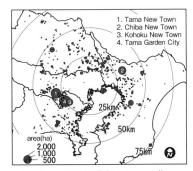

Fig. 1 New towns in Tokyo metropolitan area (based on "New Town List of Japan" Ministry of Land, Infrastructure and Transport)

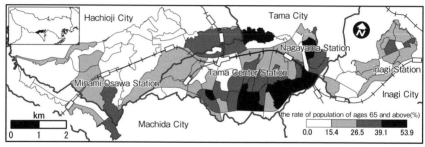

Fig. 2   The rate of aging by area in Tama New Town (based on the National Population Census 2015)

ity such as elderly people.

Deterioration of buildings is also progressing in the early occupancy area. As there are many slopes and stairs in the hilly area and many apartments are not equipped with elevators, barrier-free environment for elderly people is also an ongoing challenge.

●New Town regeneration initiative   In response to the current situation, many efforts have been made to regenerate the Tama New Town considering both hard and soft aspects of the issues.

Housing and infrastructure reconstruction has been conducted to cope with the hard aspect of the issues. The first project targeted the reconstruction of the housing complex in Suwa area (2010–2013). The idea of this remodeling became a topic for the time in the late 1980's and it had to overcome various difficulties, especially with the homeowners association, before it became a reality. The mid-rise apartments without elevators (23 buildings, 640 units) were transformed into a modern high-rise apartment complex (7 buildings, 1,249 units) equipped with elevators and security devices as well as nursery, day care services and medical clinics. New housing units attracted the young generation and eased the aging of the community. Reconstruction of public housing is also carried out in the Suwa-

Nagayama area on the lands of abandoned schools.

Provision of nursing care and community services, and the creation of community spaces such as community cafes and salons using the vacant shops in the shopping streets can be seen as the current actions towards the betterment of the soft issues. Residents of the new town play a leading role in the regeneration efforts (Ref. 1). In Nagayama, a Comprehensive Community Support Center, which is the base for community welfare, was established in the middle of the shopping street. The Center closely works with the residents who are actively involved in the new town revival.

●Conclusion to stand a new town

Development of Tama New Town has been a long-term project. Consequently, the housing designs and age composition of the residents as well as the community issues are different in each occupancy area. We mainly introduced the current situation of the early occupancy area of the new town. Tama New Town can get labeled as an "Old Town" if we look at only one side of its aging population. Tama New Town is by no means a uniform city, and we can say that the town continues to stand a "New Town".

(Hitoshi Miyazawa)

Tokyo's islands

●**Tourism boom in remote islands** Island areas such as Ogasawara Islands and Yakushima Island with unique and rich nature are recognized as attractive destinations for nature-based tourism activities in Japan. Ecotourism, which is considered as an environmentally sensitive form of tourism, is particularly thriving in the island areas recently.

Prior to the recent popularity and expansion of ecotourism, a phenomenon called "Remote Islands Escape" had occurred in the island areas during the high economic growth period of Japan. In particular, the Izu Islands of Tokyo became a popular tourist resort for young people as a result of the tourism boom. However, Izu Oshima Island was the only known tourist destination in the Izu Islands at that time. The history of tourism in Izu Oshima goes back to the Meiji era. In the following section, we explain the history of the tourism development in the Izu Islands based on the representative example of Izu Oshima Island.

●**Tourism development in the Izu Islands** The Izu Islands were a place of banishment until the Edo period, and normal people were not allowed to visit there. It was opened to the general public after the establishment of a sea route in 1907 under the order of the Tokyo governor. Tourism development began in earnest after the world economic depression in 1928. As the revenue received from the cargo vessels was not enough to operate the Tokyo Bay Kisen (now Tokai Kisen), a new route connecting Tokyo, Oshima and Shimoda also opened. Several artworks were published in the opening year of the new route, including a song titled "Habu

no minato" and a short story by the famous novelist Kawabata Yasunari titled "The Izu Dancer". Many people got to know about the Izu Oshima Island through these creative works (Fig. 1). On the other hand, Mt. Mihara, an active volcano on the Izu Oshima Island, was frequently introduced on media as a suicide hotspot. A female university student has committed suicide by jumping off the crater of Mt. Mihara in 1933. The incident influenced a series of suicide incidents by young people at the same place. However, all these incidents increased the publicity of the island and the number of visitors to Izu Oshima increased year by year.

Hiking at Mt. Mihara was the mainstream tourism in Izu Oshima in the early Showa era, and there were more than 10 teahouses from the first station to the summit in 1935. A jetty was constructed in the present Motomachi port in 1939 to operate large ferries, and the development of Oshima as a tourist resort was progressing smoothly. However, tourism in Izu Oshima temporarily stagnated due to World War II.

Tourism started to develop again in 1949 after World War II ended. The opening of the Oshima Airport and road maintenance were carried out in 1963. The regional development of the Izu Islands in the 1960s and 70s was centered on Izu Oshima's tourism development.

Since the mid-1960s, the other islands of Izu started to get popular especially among young people. Hachijojima was the first area where tourism development progressed. A tourist association and a large hotel were established in 1959 on Hachijojima Island, and in 1960, a tourist bus service started after the opening of an airport and development of roads (Fig. 2). Sometime later, tourism development was carried out on Miyakejima Island. By 1965, accessibility improved in Miyakejima by establishing two ports. Port facilities and guesthouses were established in the second half of 1960 on the islands of Niijima and Kozushima.

●**Causes and Impact of Remote Island Boom**   Since the remote island boom, tourism-oriented industries such as lodging have become a key economic activity in the Izu Islands. In Niijima and Kozushima, agriculture and fisheries were the main economic activity until around 1960. However, revenue from tourism industry such as guesthouses increased significantly as a result of the tourism boom (Ref. 1, 2).

One of the main causes for the tourism boom in remote islands was the impact of the Remote Island Development Act enacted in 1953. Infrastructure in the island areas improved through the development of port facilities and airports enabling easy access for tourists. On the other hand, camping became popular among young people in the 1960s, and the Izu Islands became an attractive destination to enjoy the outdoors. Therefore, the remote island boom was a result of several social and cultural backgrounds. Today, nature-based tourism such as geotourism in Izu Oshima and dolphin watching in Mikurajima are among the most popular types of tourism on the Izu Islands (Fig. 3).   (Kantaro Takahashi)

Fig. 1   The Habu no Minato in Izu Oshima, a lively port before World War II (photo by Toshio Kikuchi in June 2011)

Fig. 2   Hachijojima Island, developed as a tourism attraction after World War II (photo by Toshio Kikuchi in September 2011)

Fig. 3   The crater of Mt. Mihara, one of the highlights of Izu Oshima geo tourism (photo by Toshio Kikuchi in May 2015)

Tokyo's subway system

●**A gigantic and complex underground network**   Underground Tokyo, there is a huge subway network extending over 300 km around the Yamanote Line, with underground passages connecting the subway stations, subway exits and the buildings above.   About 10 million people ride the subway every day (Tokyo Metro 9 lines and Toei Subway 4 lines).   The subway was constructed as a social infrastructure to meet the requirements of Tokyo metropolitan area, which is home to about 38 million people.

●**First subway opening**   Asia's first subway line opened in 1927 between Asakusa and Ueno by the Tokyo Underground Railway Company (Ref. 1).   People hoped for a new railway as an alternative transport to the horse tramway that connected Shimbashi, the railhead, and Asakusa, the downtown area at the time.   Hayakawa Noritsugu, known as the "father of the subway in Tokyo," went on an inspection tour of London underground and realized the necessity of having a similar raiway system in Tokyo. Consequently, he started the construction of a subway between Asakusa and Shimbashi. A short distance operation was first opened between Asakusa and Ueno due to the financial difficulties.   The operation was extended to Shimbashi in 1934 with financial assistance from department stores along the railway line. The station was named "Mitsukoshi-mae" as the construction cost of the station was born by the Mitsukoshi Department Store.

On the other hand, Tokyo High-speed Rail Corporation opened a subway from Shibuya to Shimbashi in 1939. In the same year they started direct operation between Asakusa

and Shibuya, which was the origin of the current Ginza Line. With the establishment of the Teito Rapid Transit Authority, the predecessor of the Tokyo Metro, in 1941, the Japanese Government took over the management of the Ginza Line.

●**Construction of Marunouchi Line under severe financial pressure**   The population movement from old downtown to Yamanote in the postwar years increased the number of commuters from the western suburbs to the central Tokyo, and congestion on the JNR Chuo Line was an issue.   The Marunouchi Line was planned as the first postwar subway, and the section between Ikebukuro and Ochanomizu opened in 1954. In an era of financial hardship, the route around Yotsuya and Korakuen was constructed above the ground to control the construction cost.

The Ginza and Marunouchi Lines use the third rail system, a method in which power is supplied through rigid conductors placed along the side tracks, and there are no pantographs on the roof.   As a result, the two subway lines cannot be interoperated with other subway lines.

● **Mutual direct operation of the railways** In the 1960s, advanced economic growth led to the development of suburban housing such as New Town Development, accelerating the concentration of commuter flows to the city center.   In 1956, the Urban Transport Council's first report indicated that the suburban commuter rails and subways were conducting a mutual direct operation.   This mutual direct operation has supported the development of the present Tokyo (Ref. 2).

At the beginning mutual direct operation

was planned for three railway lines; Keihin Electric Express Railway, Toei Asakusa Line and Keisei Electric Railway. Since the track width of Keihin Electric Express Railway was the same standard gauge (1,435 mm) as Shinkansen, Toei Asakusa Line was built by the standard gauge, and the track width of Keisei Electric Railway was improved to match the standard gauge. The first mutual direct operation was realized in 1960. The Toei Asakusa Line and subsequent subways use the pantagraph method to collect electricity instead of the third rail system as in Ginza and Marunouchi Lines, in order to match the connecting railways.

The Hibiya Line started direct operation with Tobu railway at Kitasenju Station in 1962, which was the first mutual direct operation of the subway lines under the Tokyo Metro. Tokyo Metro, has implemented mutual direct operation with all the subsequent lines including Tozai, Chiyoda (Fig. 1), Hanzomon, Yurakucho, Namboku and Fukutoshin Lines.

The Toei Shinjuku Line carries out mutual direct operation with the Keio Line, Toei Mita Line carries it out with the Tokyu Meguro Line. The track width of Toei Mita Line is a narrow gauge (1,067 mm) similar to the Tokyo Metro lines. However, the Toei Shinjuku Line has a track width of 1,372 mm to match the Keio Line. Since the 3 lines of Toei Subway (Asakusa, Mita, Shinjuku Lines) have different track sizes, it has been difficult to implement mutual direct operation. At the same time, the Toei Oedo Line uses the "linear metro method" driven by magnetism to reduce its construction costs, and mutual direct operation with other railways is not possible.

●**Mastering the Tokyo's subway** There are some challenges associated with the management of this huge subway network of Tokyo (Fig. 2). The fares differ between Tokyo Metro and Toei Subway, and the transfer is complicated, especially for foreign tourists. In recent years, IC cards have been introduced, and in addition to station exits and timetables, information on transfer routes and train location can be obtained in real time on the Internet. By using such technologies one can be master riding multiple Tokyo subways. (Hitoshi Yagai)

Fig. 1 Subway entrance of the Chiyoda Line (near Yoyogi Uehara Station) (photo by Hitoshi Yagai in April 2019)

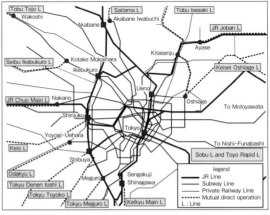

Fig. 2 Tokyo subway network and shared operational areas

Chapter 7 Tokyo's Economy

A commercial facility built on the former site of a shipbuilding site in Toyosu, making use of the docks at the shipyard (photo by Naoto Yabe in June 2017)

The economy of Tokyo metropolitan area has undergone significant changes, since the 1990s. Among various vital aspects of economy, this chapter focuses on the changes in industrial structure by analyzing the land use changes in the Tokyo metropolitan area.

7.1 Land use changes in the Tokyo metropolitan area since the 1990s

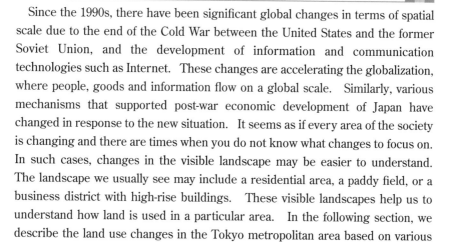

Since the 1990s, there have been significant global changes in terms of spatial scale due to the end of the Cold War between the United States and the former Soviet Union, and the development of information and communication technologies such as Internet. These changes are accelerating the globalization, where people, goods and information flow on a global scale. Similarly, various mechanisms that supported post-war economic development of Japan have changed in response to the new situation. It seems as if every area of the society is changing and there are times when you do not know what changes to focus on. In such cases, changes in the visible landscape may be easier to understand. The landscape we usually see may include a residential area, a paddy field, or a business district with high-rise buildings. These visible landscapes help us to understand how land is used in a particular area. In the following section, we describe the land use changes in the Tokyo metropolitan area based on various land use maps that are often used in geographical studies.

Factory closure Globalization of business functions has led to a decrease in the number of factories in Tokyo. For example, factory closure can happen when a domestic factory moves to Asia where labor costs are low. In addition, domestic factories may be integrated or closed as a result of corporate mergers or business reevaluations. Let's take a look at the land use change from 1994 to 2014 to see the places where such factory closures occurred in the Tokyo metropolitan area.

Fig. 7.1 compares the factory land in 1994 and 2014. In this figure, land use is divided into rectangular meshes with a side length of approximately 100 m. There are many places where land use has changed drastically, especially in the city center. Most of the factories have changed to other land uses in Koto and Edogawa Wards on the east side of the city center. For example, in Koto Ward, the shipyard of IHI (Ishikawajima-Harima Heavy Industries) in Toyosu facing Tokyo Bay has been converted to some high-rise office buildings, condominiums, and commercial facilities. At the same time, many factories are changing to other land uses in Shinagawa Ward, Ota Ward, and Kawasaki City (in Kanagawa Prefecture) in the area southwest of the city center. For example, the former sites of NEC Corporation and other factories in Musashi Kosugi in Kawasaki City have been transformed into a popular residential area with high-rise condominiums.

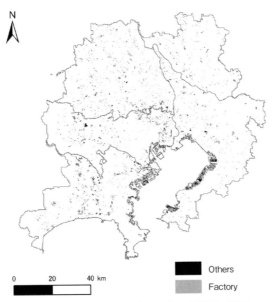

Fig. 7.1   Factory land change from 1994 to 2014
Based on the grid land-use data by the Geospatial Information Authority of Japan and digital national land information by the Ministry of Land, Infrastructure and Transport.

On the other hand, land uses for factories in 1994 remains the same in 2014 in the suburbs away from the city center. In particular, large factories are often used for the same purposes. However, there are cases that the land use is classified under "factory" even if it has changed to a logistics facility. For example, the Ebara Corporation near Haneda Airport has been changed to a logistics facility of Yamato Transport. However, it is still classified under "factory". We also could find certain changes in the site of former Nissan Motors' Murayama factory in the Tama area of Tokyo. A part of the site is occupied by a branch of AEON Company shopping mall, but the other parts remain vacant.

Let's calculate the percentage of changes in land use under factories from 1994 to 2014. 49% of the land use under factories in 1994 remains the same in 2014. In other words, about half of the factories in the Tokyo metropolitan area have changed to other land use over the past 20 years. However, as mentioned earlier, there are fewer manufacturing factories in operation as some land uses classified under factories are logistic facilities at present. 25% of total factory lands have been transformed in to low-rise buildings. 11% of the total factory lands have changed to vacant land or wasteland. This is considered as "temporary land use" before changing to another land use. 5% of former factory lands accounts for high-rise buildings. Changes from factories to high-rise buildings tend to be concentrated near the city center, such as Koto Ward (the area includes a large number of high-rise condominiums).

Changes in farmland   Next, let's look at changes in farmland as another land use change. Fig. 7.2 shows the farmland change from 1994 to 2014. At first glance, it can be seen that farmlands have undergone less change than factories and statistically, 69% of the farmlands remain under the same classification in 2014. Only about 23% of farmlands have changed to low-rise buildings, which indicates that the urban sprawling has declined after the collapse of the bubble economy, and there is a new trend of returning to the city center. However, certain farmlands continue to be urbanized.

Let's take a look at the large size farmlands that have changed to other land uses. In some parts of Kisarazu City in Chiba Prefecture, where the Tokyo Bay Aqua Line passes, farmlands have been converted into an outlet mall. In Koshigaya City, Saitama Prefecture, there is a place that has changed from farmland to a large shopping mall (AEON Lake Town).

There are also places that are influenced by the newly established transportation facilities. Around Tsukuba Express stations in Ibaraki Prefecture, which opened in 2005, a large plot of farmland was converted into a town. At the same time, some changes can be found in the farmlands around the newly developed express way interchanges, such as the Ken'O Express way and the outer ring road. Industrial parks with factories and logistics facilities are built in the vicinity of the interchanges.

Declining and growing industries   As described in the previous sections, we have looked at the land use changes from 1994 to 2014, focusing on factories and farmlands. There was a significant change in factories as more than half of the factories in the Tokyo metropolitan area were gone by 2014. Some factories have moved overseas. The number of manufacturing sites, which had a large presence in the industry, is decreasing. On the other hand, we found that the creation of large-scale commercial facilities and logistics facilities is the common factor in factory and farmland change. One main reason for the expansion of logistics facilities is the increase in online sales. The Internet-related businesses are attracting attention as a growing industry in recent years.

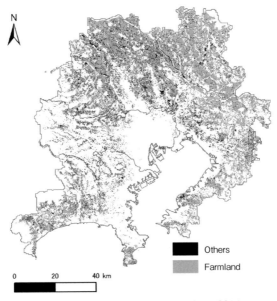

Fig. 7.2 Farmland change from 1994 to 2014
Based on the grid land-use data by the Geospatial Information Authority of Japan and digital national land information by the Ministry of Land, Infrastructure and Transport.

7.2 Location of IT industries in the Tokyo metropolitan area

The development of information and communication technology has been expanding globally since the 1990s, particularly the IT (information technology) industry.   The IT industry can also be considered as a service industry for business establishments that provide services for companies.   For example, when you make a reservation for an air ticket, you may make an online reservation, a system developed by the IT industry.   Airline companies use professional IT companies to create reservation systems for them.   It is worth checking where these IT companies are located.

Location of IT companies   Fig. 7.3 shows the number of persons engaged in the IT industry in 2014, divided into meshes with a side length of approximately 500 m.   To get a clear idea about the growing industry, it would have been better if we could see the changes in the number of persons engaged since the 1990s.   However, since the method of corporate statistical survey has changed, it is difficult to directly compare changes over a period of time. Therefore, only the distribution in 2014 is shown in Fig. 7.3.

As you can see from the figure, the IT industry is remarkably concentrated in the city center.   Locations are mainly found in the central three wards and also in the sub-centers of Shinjuku and Shibuya (Fig. 7.4).   You can see that there are some companies in the suburbs, such as Yokohama, but there is a significant difference compared to the concentration in the city center.   While manufacturing factories were widely distributed in the suburbs of the Tokyo metropolitan area, the IT industry is not located in the suburbs.   What could be the reason for this particular distribution?

Previous studies (Ref. 1, 2) point out that face-to-face contact is important to carry out the work effectively in the IT industry.   For example, when developing a reservation system, it is necessary to have direct communication between the customer and the IT company to effectively discuss the requirements.   Even though there are other communication methods such as e-mails and video calls, these tools are considered less effective compared to the amount of flexibility, and one can gain detailed specifications through face-to-face contact with the customer.   As a result, the IT companies are mainly located in the central Tokyo area near their customer base.

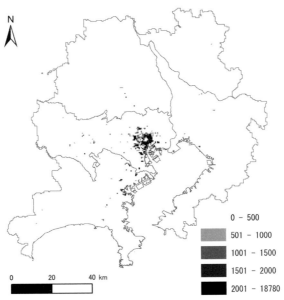

Fig. 7.3 The number of persons engaged in information and communications industry in the Tokyo metropolitan area (2014)

Based on the Economic Census by the Ministry of Internal Affairs and Communications.

0 - 500
501 - 1000
1001 - 1500
1501 - 2000
2001 - 18780

Fig. 7.4 Redevelopment work progressing around Shibuya Station (photo by Naoto Yabe in November, 2019)

A globally famous IT company has moved into the right high rise building.

7.3　Changes in industrial structure

In this chapter, we focused on the land use changes in the Tokyo metropolitan area mainly from the 1990s to the 2010s. By looking at the land use changes, we could identify that the manufacturing factories have declined by more than half. The trend of deindustrialization commonly seen in developed countries seems to be no exception in the Tokyo metropolitan area. We also found the creation of large-scale commercial facilities and logistics facilities as a common factor associated with the land use changes in the former factory sites and farmlands. Even though the manufacturing industry is declining, the IT industry is growing as a service industry. A main characteristic of the IT industry is its location, which tends to concentrate predominantly in the city center.

The main characteristics of the industrial structure change in the Tokyo metropolitan area over the past 20 years is the decline of manufacturing industry and the growth of IT industry. At the same time, business services such as legal services, accounting, and marketing have also grown. The main customer base of these business services is the central management division of companies, which is often located at the head offices. Therefore, the demand for business services in the Tokyo area where the head offices are largely concentrated has been significantly increasing. Such changes in the industrial structure have been discussed for major global cities (Ref. 3, 4). These changes have been expanding in Tokyo since the 1990s.

Looking at the spatial changes in the industrial structure, the manufacturing factories have declined significantly in and around the city center, while the IT industry has grown there. Changes in the industrial structure are strongly visible in and around the city center. On the other hand, the spaces related to production in the suburbs, such as factories and farmlands, have changed to spaces related to consumption, such as commercial facilities or logistics facilities that support the distribution of goods. While large-scale shopping malls and outlet malls in the suburbs are gaining popularity, department stores at the suburban stations are increasingly closing. This type of change in old and new commercial facilities is a common phenomenon that can be seen in regional cities. At the same time, population trends in Tokyo and regional cities in Japan also show a similar pattern. In Tokyo's case, some suburban cities have experienced population decrease, which is similar to the regional cities. The depopulation trend of the suburban cities may lead to a similar phenomenon facing the regional cities in Japan. Therefore, it would be highly important to look at the changes in the city through various aspects (Ref. 5) to understand the process that shapes the future.

(Naoto Yabe)

Ginza in Tokyo

●**Two types of Ginza** There are two types of "Ginza" in Tokyo. One is the renowned commercial area from Ginza 1-chome to 8-chome (referred to as prestigious Ginza here). The other type represents the shopping streets that have incorporated the name "Ginza" (referred to as shopping street here). Although these shopping streets have distinctive characteristics, both types have become important commercial areas in Tokyo today.

●**History and urban transformation of Ginza** Ginza was originally a rural area located at the edge of the Edo Maetō peninsula. The Edo *shogun* transferred his silver-coin mint to the area from Sumpu in 1612 and established various relevant businesses. As a result, Ginza was urbanized as a townsmen district where craftsmen and merchants lived. The place name is taken from the silver mint (Ginza). After the Great Fire of Meireki in 1657, commercial functions increased as many shops were rebuilt facing the streets, and Ginza developed as one of the most important commercial areas of Edo (Ref. 1).

Western culture and trends became popular in Ginza in the Meiji era with the influence of a foreign settlement in Tsukiji to the east of Ginza. The opening of Shimbashi station on the south side also improved access to the international city of Yokohama. In 1872, a large fire broke out in the Ginza area and the buildings facing the Ginza Street were rebuilt in Georgian style creating the so-called Ginza-*renga-gai*. Ginza-*renga-gai* has developed commercial functions such as cafes and beer halls, and shop windows at stores to display merchandise adopting the

Western culture. Pavements and gaslights were also installed creating a rare ambience at the time. People were increasingly attracted to see this sophisticated space with elements of Western culture.

Later, in the Taisho era, the brick street disappeared in the Great Kanto Earthquake and Ginza transformed into a modern commercial area with buildings exhibiting neon signs. After World War II, many company showrooms gathered in the area, and Ginza was popularly introduced as a commercial destination on various media. Expensive jewellery and high-end brand shops have been expanding since the 1970s and Ginza grew into a big commercial area with upscale boutiques, brand shops and Michelin star restaurants. In this way, Ginza changed from a townsmen district in the Edo period to a brick town in the Meiji era, turning into an attractive commercial area for people to admire, and an upscale brand of luxury commercial land with prestigious Ginza at present (Fig. 1).

●**Tokyo's shopping streets** There is another type of "Ginza" shopping streets in Tokyo that creates a bustle different from the atmosphere of the prestigious Ginza shopping street. The beginning of this type of "Ginza" shopping streets is said to be Togoshi Ginza shopping street in Shinagawa Ward, Tokyo (Fig. 2). Togoshi area often suffered from poor drainage in the streets in the past. To overcome the issue, paved streets were built in the shopping street out of the brick debris from Ginza generated by the Great Kanto Earthquake. The shopping street was named Togoshi Ginza in the hope that it will prosper as a representative commercial area in Tokyo same as the prestigious Ginza (Fig. 2). Since then, increasing number of similar shopping streets incorporated the name "Ginza" throughout the country, and there are currently about 90 shopping streets in Tokyo alone. The famous shopping streets are also featured on TV, magazines and other media. Togoshi Ginza (in Shinagawa Ward), Jujo Ginza (in Kita Ward) and Sunamachi Ginza (in Koto Ward) are the three well-known "Ginza" shopping streets in Tokyo.

For local people, these "Ginza" shopping streets are regular markets where they can shop for daily necessities. On the other hand, Ginza shopping streets are popular tourist spots for visitors where they can enjoy the atmosphere of downtown areas while tasting the street food varieties at the stores lining the streets. Due to the increasing popularity among tourists, many travel agencies also include Ginza shopping streets in Tokyo in tour packages nowadays. These Ginza shopping streets bring people the pleasure of "seeing" uncommon spaces and also the pleasure of "buying" and "dining" in commonly used spaces at the same time. In other words, the "Ginza" shopping streets are typical examples of the transformation of regular spaces into tourist destinations and show the great tourism potential of common spaces particularly in attracting international tourists.

●**The rise and fall of the "Ginza" shopping streets**　However, some shopping streets are shrinking due to the entry of large supermarkets and shopping malls in the vicinity. In particular, the individual speciality stores in the shopping streets get negatively affected when chain stores enter the shopping districts. Therefore, with the cooperation of local shopping associations, NPO organizations, local residents, etc., Tokyo now actively makes efforts to secure customers by creating shopping streets with unique concepts and effectively accommodating vacant stores. The three successful shopping streets in Tokyo have made the best use of the land characteristics of the respective areas, which can be identified as the key to success and sustainability of any shopping street. The two types of Ginza will continue to be the representative models of eminent and diverse commercial areas of Tokyo.

(Ryo Iizuka)

Fig. 1　Bustling Ginza (photo by Ryo Iizuka in May 2019)

Fig. 2　Bustling Togoshi Ginza (photo by Ryo Iizuka in May 2019)

Urban farming in Tokyo

●**Farming in the city**   Tokyo comprises a mixture of urban and rural land uses. Along with the urban land uses such as high-rise buildings, commercial facilities and houses, rural land uses remain in the form of urban and suburban farming.

In recent years, urban farming is considered as a way to create rural spaces in the immediate vicinity of urban residents. In particular, urban farmlands become green spaces and also leisure spaces for people to relax. Agricultural lands have also become evacuation sites in the event of disasters, and their multifaceted functions have been increasingly recognized. In 2015, the Basic Law on the Promotion of Urban Agriculture, which highlights the importance of urban-farming for a good urban environment, was enacted.

●**History of urban farming in Tokyo**
The origins of urban farming in Tokyo date back to the Edo period. The population in Edo increased rapidly due to the inflow of workers engaged in the reconstruction of Edo Castle and urban development, or due to alternative working system of feudal lords (*sankin-kotai*). To cope with the rapidly increasing population, the shogunate encouraged the cultivation of rice and wheat in the rural areas, and vegetables in the suburbs. As a result, suburban agriculture, centering on the cultivation of green vegetables and root crops, developed around Edo.

After the Meiji era, suburbanization progressed along with the development of railway lines, and in the Taisho era, the tendency further strengthened due to the reconstruction work after the Great Kanto Earthquake. Farmlands gradually changed into residential lands in the process of suburbanization. After World War II, farmlands were rapidly converted to urban land use such as residential, industrial, and commercial lands due to housing shortages and population concentration in Tokyo during the period of high economic growth. However, some farmers and farmlands survived in urban situations and contributed to the emergence of the current form of urban farming in Tokyo.

●**Characteristics of urban farming in Tokyo**   The distinctive feature of Tokyo's urban farming is its close proximity to consumers and the ability to easily meet the needs of consumers (Ref. 1). There are two farm management approaches that enable the fulfilment of urban demand. One approach focuses on direct sales of agricultural products through farm-stands and shops of agricultural cooperative associations (such as JA). The other focuses on recreational farming by offering tourism farms and farming-experience gardens.

In Tokyo, direct sales of agricultural product are largely concentrated in the Tama area, such as Tachikawa and Kodaira Cities. These farmers use small farmlands of about 1ha to grow small volumes of green vegetables such as spinach and Japanese mustard spinach (*komatsuna*), root vegetables such as radish and carrot, or fruits such as Japanese pears and blueberries (Fig. 1). Many farmers generally grow about 30 types of crops annually, but some also manage to grow 50 to 60 types of crops. Farmers who conduct direct sales can meet the needs of urban residents by making annual sales plans based on seasonal demand patterns and carrying out multi-item small-volume production.

On the other hand, recreational farming is actively conducted in the outer fringe of the city such as Nerima and Setagaya Wards. In Nerima Ward, farming-experience gardens where users can take classes on farming from farmers are becoming popular among urban residents. There, the farms are used as a means of learning farm work to grow fresh and safe crops or for children's education and leisure purposes (Fig. 2). Farming-experience gardens are different from community gardens, and the usage fee is directly paid to the farmers. At the same time, farming-experience gardens are recog-nized as a form of agriculture management and there is a merit for farmers such as ex-emption from inheritance tax. Since mainly farmers operate these farming-experience gardens, new communities tend to be formed around such farms. In other words, the farming-experience gardens become im-mediate rural spaces for urban residents.

● **The future of urban farming in Tokyo**

Although urban farming in Tokyo is greatly influenced by urbanization, it has survived by taking advantage of close proximity and in-teraction with urban residents. In recent years, young farmers who earn high profits from contracted cultivation with famous restaurants have given much hope for fu-ture. Their speciality is the cultivation of traditional vegetables of Edo period and vari-eties of foreign vegetables. Many of these young farmers are former employees of pri-vate companies and already have manage-ment experience. They develop their farm-ing methods by constantly obtaining advanced and latest information on farm management. Their presence also bright-ens the future of urban farming in Tokyo.

(Ryo Iizuka)

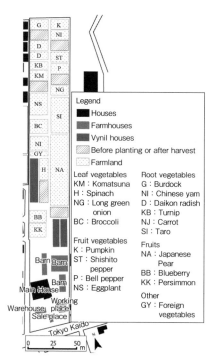

Fig. 1 Ground usage of farmers conducting direct sales in Kodaira City (modified after Ref. 1)

Fig. 2 A farming-experience garden in Nerima Ward (photo by Ryo Iizuka in September 2009)

Harajuku backstreets and fashion

● **Harajuku backstreets (Ura-Harajuku)**

Ura-Harajuku consists of the back alleys off the main streets in Harajuku. Precisely, it is just one street off Omotesando and Meiji Streets (Fig. 1). The central area of Ura-Harajuku is located along the road called Cat Street, which is the culvert of the Shibuya River that flows through the area. As shown in the figure, Ura-Harajuku area runs 500 m east from Harajuku Station extending straight from southwest to northeast direction until it crosses Meiji Street. Ura-Harajuku boasts a concentration of top-level apparel retailers in Tokyo, and it is a popular area where many fashion-loving young people gather. Ura-Harajuku attracts widespread attention from both within Japan and overseas. Many international designers and tourists visit the area to see the latest fashion trends.

● **Concentration of clothing retail stores in Ura-Harajuku** Since the mid-1990s, fashion-related stores have largely gathered in Ura-Harajuku. In particular, a store that lined up clothes made by a young designer gained enormous attention from people and greatly contributed to the Ura-Harajuku's popularity all over the country. The shop opening of this young designer has initially triggered the concentration of retail stores in Ura-Harajuku. The young designer has received support from a senior designer who had been leading Harajuku's fashion industry since the 1970s. Ura-Harajuku does not face the main streets, and the low rent of the stores seems to be a favorable condition for young designers to open stores there. Following the success of the young designer's store, many other clothing stores also

started to appear in the area, resulting in a large concentration of clothing retails stores.

● **Apparel business planning** Many of the stores in Ura-Harajuku are small and medium-sized shops that are planning apparel business by themselves. When planning apparel businesses, one must first decide on a fashion design. Consumer gathering in Ura-Harajuku plays an important role in the decision-making process of the designers.

According to the interview survey with the stores, many respondents said that they "refer the clothes of people who are walking the streets of Ura-Harajuku" in deciding fashion designs (Ref. 1). In this way, designers can get good ideas and hints that help them in designing completely new combinations of colors and patterns that they have never thought of before.

Consumers of Ura-Harajuku are sensitive to their fashion especially when they go out to places where fashion lovers gather such as Ura-Harajuku. They are highly conscious about other people's eyes and pay careful attention to present themselves in the best fashion possible. In other words, Ura-Harajuku receives consumers with sophisticated and trendy fashion sense. Therefore, consumers' fashion styles are considered as a valuable source of information when deciding a new clothing design.

● **Apparel manufacturing** How do apparel retailers manufacture after deciding on a design? In Ura-Harajuku, there seems to be some stores where the designers themselves produce clothes in small quantities, but many seem to use trading companies for the manufacturing process. Trading companies generally order the apparel manufacturing process including cutting and sewing from overseas garment factories.

There is an area near Ura-Harajuku where such trading companies are concentrated. As you can see in the Fig. 1, clothing wholesale industry is gathered in the northeast area of Harajuku Station. Designers and trading company representatives should meet directly to discuss about the apparel production. Therefore, trading companies tend to gather near the retail stores to effectively facilitate their business discussions and interactions with retail stores. Ura-Harajuku and its surroundings comprise business functions from fashion designing to production mediation respectively.

●**Future prospects** If you walk through the streets of Ura-Harajuku today, you will understand that the land prices have soared, and not many young designers often open stores there as before. On the other hand, Japanese fashion brand stores that target international tourists are also prominent.

The young population in Japan is shrinking and Japan is faced with an aging population. Therefore, it would be necessary to attract overseas fashion enthusiasts and use their fashion sense in apparel planning in the future. (Naoto Yabe)

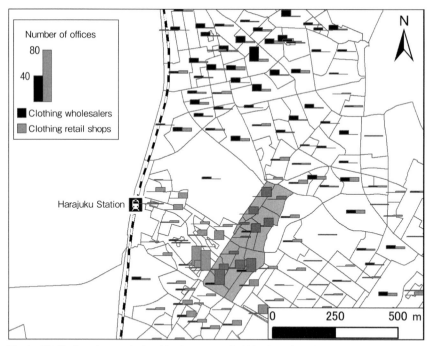

Fig. 1 Distribution of apparel-related businesses around Harajuku (based on the Economic Census by the Ministry of Internal Affairs and Communications)

Close-up

Machi-kōba in Tokyo

●**What is a "*machi-kōba*"?** As you walk through the streets of Tokyo, you may find small factories including sheet metal processing and metal polishing workshops in residential areas. These small factories in the urban areas are often called *machi-kōba*. *Machi-kōba* has been developed under a subcontracting scheme with large companies particularly for manufacturing machinery and automobile components.

However, with the transformation of industrial structure and development of high technology and globalization at the same time, a significant change can be seen in the subcontracting scheme between the small factories and large companies. Recently, *machi-kōba* is also featured in novels and TV dramas, and people are increasingly becoming interested in learning about the small factories.

●**Development of *machi-kōba***

Unfortunately, there is no precise data on the number of small factories in Tokyo. However, the number can be estimated to some extent from the industrial statistical surveys (Fig. 1). According to the statistical surveys, as of 2016, there were 29,615 manufacturers in Tokyo, of which 27,126, or 91.6 %, were small enterprises with 19 or fewer employees. Arguably, small factories support many manufacturers in Tokyo.

Looking at the number of manufacturing companies in each municipality in 2017, the top five are Ota, Adachi, Sumida, Edogawa and Katsushika Wards. These wards are located in downtown areas, where small and medium-scale enterprises are concentrated and many *machi-kōba* are located. In particular, Ota Ward, which has 1,200 factories, is recognized as the "town of *machi-kōba*".

In Ota Ward, since the Great Kanto Earthquake, industrial land has been developed through consolidation of arable lands. The machinery industry developed taking advantage of munitions production for World War II and the Korean War. However, due to the end of the war, the accompanying economic downturn and the changes in subcontract manufacturing of large companies, many small factories faced a severe blow and struggled to maintain a certain scale of production, which led to a series of bankruptcies in 1960.

Under such circumstances, craftsmen who came from the provinces and had acquired apprentice through mass employment in the 1950s became independent workers and became key actors of the future of small industries. This became possible since large-scale equipment was not necessary to run the production due to technological advances related to factory equipment. Space could be acquired because the seaweed drying grounds were converted to factory lands at that time. The number of small factories called "One-master factories" run by independent apprentices increased rapidly (Ref. 1).

In one-master factories, specialized machine parts have been produced by the apprentices using their own skills, technology acquired by years of experience. Since each factory has specialized technology, a production network between the factories has been formed. The area where the individual factories are grouped functions as if it were one large factory. Such an increase in the number of small factories and the formation of production networks continued until the

1980s, when Ota Ward was recognized as the "town of *machi-kōba*" (Fig. 2).

● **Small factory decline** The collapse of the bubble economy in the 1990s and the accompanying recession had a major impact on the operation of small factories in Ota Ward. Large enterprises had to reduce their manufacturing costs by moving the factories overseas where labor costs were lower, resulting in a decrease in orders for the small factories. In Ota Ward, where the subcontracting with large companies and the division of labor system using the production network between small factories was the canter of production, many small factories failed to survive with the ongoing situation. In addition, the aging of the apprentices also contributed to the decrease in town factories.

Houses were built on the former factory sites, and the remaining factories have to operate in a residential environment surrounded by condominiums and apartments. For this reason, many town factories are now using machines with less noise or renovating buildings with soundproofing equipment in order to reduce disturbance to urban residents.

● **Rejuvenation of the town factories and current status** While small factories are declining, there are also companies that make efforts to create products with newly added value while taking advantage of specialized technology and the production network between factories rather than simply subcontracting the production. New business opportunities are created through collaboration with different industries and fields, including research institutions and entrepreneurs. The situation is well described in the novel *Shitamachi Rocket*, which reveals the struggles of a small factory in developing a rocket part.

In addition, there are promotional activities that help urban residents deepen their understanding of the small factories. The Ota Open Factory, which is operated in collaboration with industry, academia and government in Ota Ward, has gained popularity as an event where visitors are allowed to visit the small factories and experience production technology casually. It is necessary to gain the understanding of urban residents in order to facilitate the production of small factories. The flexibility of small factories to the changing environment can be seen as the driving force to sustain the operations of current small factories.   (Ryo Iizuka)

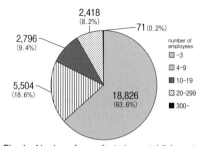

Fig. 1 Number of manufacturing establishments in Tokyo by size of business (based on Industrial statistical survey (*Totalized value for establishments with 3 or fewer employees)

Fig. 2 *Machi-kōba* area in Ota Ward (photo by Ryo Iizuka in May 2019)

Chapter 8

Tourism in Tokyo

Lively Nakamise street during the Sanja-Matsuri in Asakusa, Taito Ward

This chapter reviews the characteristics of Tokyo as a tourism destination by analyzing its tourists, tourism resources and tourism industries. The chapter also explains the expansion of MICE business in Tokyo, which is considered as an important city strategy for the future.

8.1 Tokyo's inbound tourism boom

The rise in tourists　Tokyo's inbound tourism is growing and there is an increase of both domestic and international tourist arrivals (Fig. 8.1). Since the survey standards were changed in 2009, let's take a closer look at the statistics after 2010. Domestic tourists increased from 45.7 million tourists in 2010 to 52.3 million tourists in 2017 at an increase rate of 14%. Over 90% of the domestic tourists were day-trippers and overnight stayers were fewer comparably. However, Tokyo records the highest number of overnight staying tourists in Japan when both domestic and international arrivals are calculated. According to the national statistical data issued by the Japan Tourism Agency on the type of tourism spots visited by the tourists in 2017, the majority of tourists (70%) have visited urban tourism spots, followed by sports and leisure attractions (13%) and historical or cultural sites (7%), which shows that the demand for urban tourism is particularly high.

Characteristics of international tourists　Compared to domestic tourists, international tourists are a small market representing only 1 to 3% of tourists in Tokyo. However, the number of international tourists has doubled during the period of 2010 to 2017 (from 5.94 million to 13.8 million tourists) and the increase rate alone is 132%. Inbound tourism policies and promotions by the Japanese government can be seen as a key factor for this significant growth. According to the country-based data by Japan Tourism Agency, neighboring East Asian countries such as China, Taiwan and Korea represented the highest number of tourists in 2017. Having attracted approximately 50 to 70% of international tourists who arrived in Japan in the same year, Tokyo has become one of the most sought-after tourist destinations. On the other hand, Americans were the highest among the tourists from the west. In addition to sightseeing, it is estimated that many Americans visit Tokyo for business purposes.

Tokyo as a tourism hub   Holding a huge residential population of over 13 million people and cutting-edge infrastructure such as a well-maintained railway network and conveniently-located international airports, Tokyo functions as a major tourism hub for travelers.   For example, approximately half of the domestic tourists visiting the tourist spots located in Tokyo are people living in Tokyo itself (Fig. 8.1).   Therefore, Tokyo's residents are the central consumers of Tokyo's tourism market.   Residents in Tokyo and neighboring prefectures also represent the majority of overnight visitors to other regional cities and prefectures.   Additionally, according to the Statistical Survey on Legal Migrants by the Ministry of Justice 2017, the number of overseas departures from Tokyo was 3.79 million people, the highest in Japan (21% of all departures from Japan).

8.2 Tourism resources and tourism industries

Distribution of tourism resources   Urban tourism is the most popular

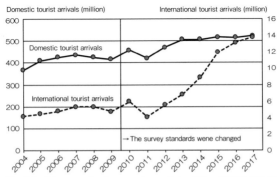

Fig. 8.1 Changes in the number of tourists visiting Tokyo (based on: Tokyo visitor survey results 2004-2017)

type of tourism in Tokyo. Yet Tokyo holds diverse tourism resources including the natural and cultural resources in Tama region and Tokyo islands. Tourism resources mean all types of resources that are usable as tourist attractions (Ref. 1). Tourism resources reflect on a particular nature and culture, and produce a special value and charm of the lands (Ref. 2). Therefore, the distribution of tourism resources is closely related to the natural and cultural environment of a particular land. Tokyo has areas with cultural resources that symbolize the

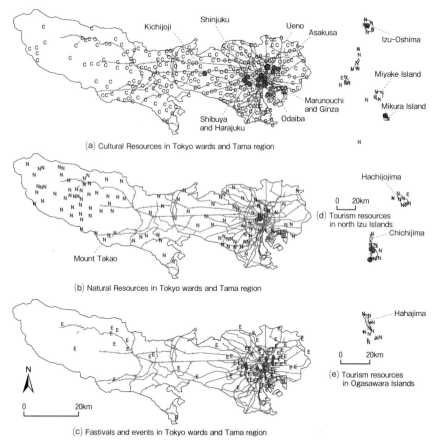

(a) Cultural Resources in Tokyo wards and Tama region

(b) Natural Resources in Tokyo wards and Tama region

(c) Fastivals and events in Tokyo wards and Tama region

(d) Tourism resources in north Izu Islands

(e) Tourism resources in Ogasawara Islands

Fig. 8.2 Distribution of tourism resources in Tokyo (based on MAPPLE's POI data and spatial data on tourism resources from the National Land Numerical Information)
C: cultural resources(POI) ●: cultural resources(A class and above), N: natural resources(POI)
●: natural resources(A class and above), E: festivals and events(POI) ◆: festivals and events(A class and above), ⊢ : railway

Tab.8.1 Tokyo's prominent tourism resources (based on spatial data on tourism resources from the National Land Numerical Information)

Cultural resources	Type
Tokyo National Museum	Museum
National Museum of Western Art	Museum
National Museum of Nature and Science	Museum
National Museum of Modern Art	Museum
Nezu Museum	Museum
Ueno Zoo	Zoo and Aquarium
Tokyo Skytree	Architecture
Tokyo Tower	Architecture
National Diet Building	Architecture
Tokyo Station	Architecture
Meiji Jingu	Shrine
Sensoji	Shrine
Harajuku	Town
Edo Castle	Castle
Shinjuku Gyoen National Garden	Park
Hama-rikyu Gardens	Park
Ghibli Museum	Theme park
Tsukiji fish market	Native landscape
Farewell ceremony of Ogasawara Islands	Native landscape
Bridges over Sumida River	Others
Ginza street	Others

Natural resources	Type
Whales in Ogasawara Islands	Animal
Dolphins in Mikurajima	Animal
Sakura in Chidorigafuchi and Ushigafuchi	Plant
Minamijima in Ogasawara Islands	Seashore
Lava fountains in Miharajima	Geology

Festivals and events	Type
Kabuki in Kabukiza	Traditional art, show and event
Sumo in Kokugikan	Traditional art, show and event
Noh-Kyōgen in National Noh Theater	Traditional art, show and event
Rakugo and other entertainments in Suehirotei	Traditional art, show and event
Kabuki and *Bunraku* in National Theater	Traditional art, show and event
Rakugo and other entertainments in Suzumoto-Engeijo	Traditional art, show and event
Hakone *Ekiden*	Traditional art, show and event
Sanja-Matsuri	Annual event

modern history and traditions as well as areas with rich natural environment, and the diversity of tourism resources spanning both culture and nature is one of the main strengths for tourism. Fig. 8.2 and Tab. 8.1 help to understand the distribution and characteristics of tourism resources in Tokyo. Here, we used the MAPPLE's POI data to cover the tourism resources as much as possible. Spatial data on tourism resources provided as one of the National Land Numerical Information was also used to indicate the representative tourism resources in Tokyo. The latter is a combination of the information on special A (the highest grade) class and normal A (the second highest grade) class tourism resources in the tourism resources inventory created by the Japan Travel Bureau Foundation and the directory of tourism sites issued by the Japan Tourism Agency. First, cultural resources are distributed largely in Tokyo's wards. Some distribution could also be found in Tama region along the railroads and in relatively closer areas to Tokyo's wards.

Tokyo's prominent tourism resources are unevenly distributed within its 23 wards. There is a vast array of prominent resources including the historical monuments such as Meiji Jingu Shrine (Shibuya Ward) and Edo Castle Ruins (Chiyoda Ward), high-rise buildings such as Tokyo Skytree (Sumida Ward), unique youth culture in Harajuku (Shibuya Ward) and Ghibli Museum (Mitaka

City).   Ueno Park in Taito Ward has outstanding cultural facilities including Ueno Zoo, Tokyo National Museum, National Science Museum, National Museum of Western Art (World Cultural Heritage).   Taito Ward also includes Asakusa, which is famous for Senso-ji temple and Kaminari-mon gate. Furthermore, festivals and events are prominent in Tokyo's 23 wards. Representative examples include Japanese traditional performing arts and sports such as *kabuki* and *sumo* wrestling, as well as annual festivals such as Sanja-Matsuri.   A wide variety of events are held in Tokyo such as fireworks festivals (*hanabi*), film festivals, seasonal flower festivals, food festivals and Christmas illuminations.

Main natural resources are those in the island areas such as the Ogasawara Islands (designated as a World Natural Heritage site) with an immense variety of wildlife and the Izu Oshima Island with geoparks such as Mt. Mihara.   There are also natural tourist spots in Tama area where you can enjoy nature experiences such as day hiking.   Mt. Takao in Hachioji City, which is also published in the Michelin Guide, records the highest number of mountain climbers in the world (Ref. 3).   Even though the natural resources are distributed widely in the islands and Tama region, a sparse distribution can also be seen within the Tokyo's wards.

Agglomeration of tourism industries in Tokyo   Tourism industry is a broad industrial field that spans the travel service sector, accommodation sector, transportation sector, food and beverage sector, entertainment sector and more. This could be a potential reason why the tourism industry has not been classified as a type of industry under the Japan's standard classification of industries by the ministry of internal affairs and communications.   Tokyo has the highest number of companies related to the tourism industry in Japan.   For example, let's look at the current situation of travel service and accommodation sectors, which are the main representatives of the tourism industry.   Travel service is a business that coordinates between travelers, accommodation facilities, railways, airlines and gains profits by providing services such as booking, travel arrangements and mediation.   Under the travel business law, travel service is classified into five types based on the scope of business; type 1 travel business, type 2 travel business, type 3 travel business, regional travel business and reseller business of tour packages.   According to the data released by the Japan Tourism Authority as of May 1, 2018, the number of travel business excluding the reselling business of tour packages throughout Japan was 9,684, of which 2,412 travel business

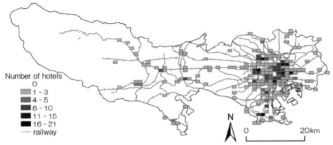

Fig. 8.3 Distribution of hotels in Tokyo's 23 wards and Tama region (based on the national mesh data of accommodation capacity)

(25%) were concentrated in Tokyo, the highest in Japan. It is about three times the value of Osaka which is the second highest in terms of concentration of travel related companies. Furthermore, 57% of the type 1 travel business is concentrated in Tokyo. The key characteristic of type 1 travel business is their ability to handle not only domestic trips but also overseas travel. The reason behind the high accumulation of type 1 travel business in Tokyo is its high demand for travel as a result of its huge residential population, scale of company concentration and its function as a global hub that connects with various countries and regions. Accommodation business is defined as sales which receives accommodation fee by providing accommodation facilities for guests under the Hotel Business Law, and the types of accommodation businesses are classified into the hotel business, the *ryokan* (Japanese style inns) business, the budget hotel business, and the lodging business. According to the Report on Public Health Administration and Services issued by the Ministry of Health, Labor and Welfare, Tokyo accommodates 718 hotels, 1306 *ryokans*, 1196 budget hotels and 13 lodges as of March 31, 2018, which is the sixth rank in the country by prefecture. However, considering only hotels, Tokyo has the highest number of hotels in Japan, especially business hotels to accommodate a large number of visitors on business trips. At the same time, international city hotels have been largely advanced into Tokyo, as it is the capital of Japan. As you can see in Fig. 8.3, hotels are unevenly distributed in Tokyo's wards. According to the Ministry of Land, Infrastructure, Transport and Tourism, Tokyo's business hotel users and city hotel users were 57% and 33% of total in the country in 2017. The annual occupancy rate is as high as 85% and 83% respectively, which clearly shows that many tourists throughout the year use hotels in Tokyo.

8.3 Expansion of MICE business in Tokyo

MICE business development strategy As globalization of the world economy advances and the international competition between cities intensifies, business events called MICE are attracting attention as a powerful tool in boosting the urban attractions. MICE is an acronym for Meeting, Incentive Travel, Convention and Exhibition. MICE business produces various values from people's gatherings and exchanges such as business opportunities, innovative ideas, high economic impact, improved international competitiveness of cities (Ref. 4).

Tokyo has been selected as a global MICE city by the Japan Tourism Agency, and various support is given to strengthen the city's competitive power in attracting international events. Further, the global MICE strategy by the Bureau of Industrial and Labor Affairs, Tokyo Metropolitan Government aims to establish a solid presence as a MICE host city and enter the world's top three cities in hosting large number of annual international conferences. Tokyo constantly strives to strengthen international ties, taking advantage of its strengths and effective use of resources, promoting cooperation with various affiliated entities, and other domestic cities (Ref. 5).

Trends in MICE Business How much MICE are being held in Tokyo? Here we look at the trends in the number of MICE business with a particular focus on international conferences. International conferences are important in strengthening the city presence. There are several types of statistical data on

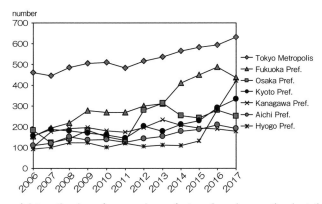

Fig. 8.4 Number of international conferences by prefecture (based on national statistics of international conferences issued by the Japan Tourism Board)

the international conferences.   We use the data provided by the specialized agencies in Japan to explore the domestic trends.   The criteria in collecting the international conference statistics by the Japan Tourism Board are 1) organizers should be international organizations/international groups or state organs and domestic organizations, 2) the total number of participants should be 50 or above, 3) participating countries should be minimum of 3 countries including Japan, 4) duration of conference should be 1 day or more.   Looking at the trends in the number of international conferences held by prefectures as shown in Fig. 8.4, it is clear that the events held within Tokyo metropolitan area have been increasing since 2006, maintaining its position as the host for the highest number of conferences nationwide.   The largest number of 631 events were recorded in 2017, of which 96% were held in Tokyo's wards.   Conferences were largely held at the University of Tokyo (67), the United Nations University (64), and the Tokyo International Forum (27).   However, the total number of participants in the University of Tokyo and the United Nations University were only around 10,000 people, whereas the Tokyo International Forum was 70,033 people. Having the largest hall capacity of about 5,000 people, the Tokyo International Forum located in Marunouchi is the main convention center in Tokyo that can attract large international conferences.

Establishment of a MICE base   Large complex facilities with integrated functions for MICE events do not exist in Tokyo as in other competing overseas cities.   Instead, the areas where certain facilities related to MICE exist are regarded as the MICE base and an environment for hosting the events has been prepared.   Currently, five areas of Marunouchi, Roppongi, Rinkaifukutoshin (the Tokyo Waterfront City), Nihonbashi and Shinagawa are designated as Tokyo's Business Events Advanced Areas.   At the same time, Hachioji City is designated as the "Tama Business Events Priority Support Area" by the Tokyo Industrial Bureau of Labor.   Each branch develops MICE-related business by effectively using the regional specific resources, and contributes to the expansion of MICE business in Tokyo.

(Koun Sugimoto)

The pandemic caused by COVID-19 at the beginning of 2020 caused Prime Minister Abe to declare the state of emergency. The tourism industry was severely affected by reluctant behaviour of people based on the stay-at-home requests during about two months. The number of foreign tourists and the number of MICE events in Tokyo have significantly decreased compared to the previous year. In order to revitalize the future tourism industry, campaigns for increasing travel demand and sustainable tourism management that include disaster countermeasures have been considered.

Two Tokyo Olympics

● Phantom Tokyo Olympics 1940   Japan erupted with joy and excitement when Tokyo won the bid to host the Olympic Games in September 2013.   Having previously hosted the 1964 Olympics, Tokyo is the first Asian city to host the Olympic Games twice.   It was actually the third time that Tokyo was chosen as the venue for the Games.   The first Olympic Games in Asia were scheduled to take place in Tokyo in 1940 as decided by IOC in July 1936, before World War II.   The event was untimely cancelled due to the Sino-Japanese War.   Even though Helsinki in Finland gained the hosting rights replacing Tokyo, the Games never took place due to the outbreak of World War II.

● Tokyo Olympics 1964   Although the 1940 Olympics were cancelled due to the war, Tokyo was again chosen as the Olympic venue at the IOC General Assembly in May 1959.   According to the Secretary General of the Tokyo Olympic Committee for Facility Construction, the difference between the Western host cities and Tokyo was "whether the fields have to be just planted or prepared all the way from plowing" (Ref. 1).   In other words, unlike the Western cities where infrastructures have been developed to a certain extent, Tokyo had enormous challenges in preparing for the Games, which included not only the construction of stadium facilities but also improving water and sewage systems and expanding road networks.   The remodeling of Tokyo for the Tokyo Olympics was planned accordingly.

Along with the development of physical infrastructure such as construction of venues for the Games and development of road networks, a city beautification movement

was carried out in 1962 aiming for a clean and attractive cityscape and increased public awareness (Ref. 2).   The stadium plan and other construction plans of the 1940 Tokyo Olympics were partly used in constructing the physical infrastructure.   For example, Komazawa Park, which was established as the second venue at the Tokyo Olympics in 1964, was the place where the main stadium (The Memorial Stadium for the 2600th year of the founding of Japan) of the Tokyo Olympics in 1940 was to be built (Fig. 1). The Tokaido Shinkansen, a high-speed railway that was launched in 1964, used the site, and the tunnel that was constructed in 1941 (Ref. 3).   Planning of the highways connecting major cities in Japan had also started during the war as "bullet roads".

The construction of the Metropolitan Expressway has transformed the landscape of central Tokyo largely.   By the development of the Metropolitan Expressway, a route connecting Haneda Airport to the Olympic venue and the athletes' village was developed.   Public lands along rivers and roads were used to minimize the land acquisitions.   The impact of the expressway on Tokyo's cityscape is still frequently debated.   The outer moat of the historical Edo Castle was reclaimed for the construction of the Expressway.   The Expressway runs above the eponymous Nihonbashi Bridge, which caused a significant change in the landscape of Nihonbashi area in Tokyo.

Former military sites were used to secure a large site for the development of the Olympic venue.   Nippon Budokan for martial arts was the site of the 1st and 2nd regiments of the Imperial Guard, Korakuen Hall for boxing and wresting was the site of Imperial Japanese Army Tokyo Arsenal, and the Yoyogi athletes village was site of the American military facilities (Ref. 3). Thus, the military sites became a venue for the Olympics, a celebration of peace, which enabled people in Tokyo as well as all over Japan to embrace a new peaceful era.

●**Changes in Tokyo toward the 2020 Tokyo Olympics and Paralympics***   2020 Tokyo Olympics and Paralympics will take over the legacy of the 1964 Olympics. The sports facilities such as the National Yoyogi Stadium and Nippon Budokan are included in the "Heritage Zone", and will be reused for the 2020 Games. The National Stadium as the main stadium has been rebuilt (Fig. 2).

On the other hand, construction of a new Olympic venue "Tokyo Bay Zone" is proceeding at a rapid pace in the Tokyo waterfront area where large-scale land reclamation can be secured. The venue will include sports facilities, the Olympic village and a press center. Therefore, in 2020, you will see a completely transformed/different landscape in Tokyo's Waterfront area.   **(Kei Ota)**

*The Tokyo 2020 Olympics and Paralympics Games are postponed to 2021 due to the COVID-19 pandemic, but the Games will still be called Tokyo 2020.

Fig. 1 Komazawa Olympic Park Athletics Stadium (right) and Olympic Monument (photo by Kei Ota in April 2019)

Fig. 2 New National Stadium has been rebuilt for the 2020 Tokyo Olympics (photo by Kei Ota in February 2020)

Tower-based tourism in Tokyo

●**History of tower-based tourism**   The debut of Eiffel Tower at the Paris exposition in 1889 changed the history of towers as religious structures. The overwhelming height of 300 m put an end to the competition among European countries to hold on their grounds the tallest buildings (Ref. 1).

The birth of observation towers in Japan dates back to 1887 when a man-made replica of Mt. Fuji was built in Asakusa in the imperial capital of Tokyo.   Built on a wooden frame covered with plaster, the replica was about 32 m in height. People could climb up the replica using the circular paths and see the real mountain from the summit.

In 1890, Ryounkaku, the 52 m tall 12-storied observatory tower opened in Asakusa. The tower was equipped with an electric elevator and soon became a landmark of the area. Unfortunately it collapsed in the Great Kanto Earthquake of 1923 (Ref. 2).   In this way, Japan was making progress in modernization in Meiji era aiming for a renewed society.   In the following section, we introduce two existing towers in Tokyo to discuss the tower-based tourism in the city.

●**Tokyo Tower**   When television broadcasting began in Japan in 1953, the television stations had to be built with their own transmission towers for broadcasting. Consequently, several independent transmission towers started to appear in the city, which caused disruption to the beauty of the cityscape.   At the same time, it was inconvenient to the public, as the direction of the television antenna had to be changed each time a channel was changed.   Tokyo Tower was born as a comprehensive broadcasting tower to solve these issues of TV broadcast-

ing.

Building the world's tallest tower (333 m) at the time surpassing the Eiffel Tower also showcased Japan's recovery from the intense shock of the defeat in World War II. The construction of the Eiffel Tower (the model of Tokyo Tower) in the 19th century also meant to repel France's humiliating defeat in the Franco-Prussian War. Tokyo Tower (under construction) appeared in the hit movie "Always: Sunset on Third Street", which was released in 2005.   The movie depicted the daily life of people in the shadow of Tokyo Tower during the period of high economic growth in Japan. Hence, the birth of Tokyo Tower symbolizes the post-war economic growth and modernization in Japan.

Cumulative total number of visitors to Tokyo Tower reached 160 million people in 2009. The highest number of annual visitors was recorded in 1959, the year after its opening (5.2 million people).   Even in 2013, more than half a century since its opening, the annual number of visitors was approximately 2.1 million, making it a leading tourist attraction representing Tokyo (Ref. 3)(Fig. 1).

●**Tokyo Skytree**   In the 21st century, Tokyo Tower was surrounded by high rising skyscrapers, and construction of a new transmission tower over 600 m of height was required for digital terrestrial television broadcasting. As a result of the competition to lure the construction site, Sumida Ward in Tokyo was chosen in 2006, and the name "Tokyo Skytree" was announced in 2008. The Tower remained undamaged from the Great East Japan Earthquake in 2011, and opened to the public in May 2012.   Unlike Tsutenkaku Tower in Osaka Prefecture and

Tokyo Tower with four-legged structures, Tokyo Skytree has a triangular base that changes to cylindrical shape at the top. The height of 634 m seems to originate from "Musashi no Kuni", which is an old administrative division consisting of Tokyo, surrounding Kanagawa Prefecture and part of Saitama Prefecture, and creates a regional image (Ref. 4). Tokyo Skytree led to an integrated development in the area. "Tokyo Skytree Town" was developed in the traditional old town style centering the Tower while modern commercial facilities "Tokyo Solamachi" was developed adjacent to the Tower.

In other words, Tokyo Skytree is not merely a tower construction, but a complex project that aimed for a new urban development by proposing a new form of tower–based tourism that allows visitors to enjoy sightseeing and shopping even without reaching the top of the Tower (Fig. 2).

Urban tourism and observation towers

The current towers are not only the landmarks of the city but also a highlight of urban tourism in Tokyo. Observation towers are prominent structures that represent urban prospects. At the same time, such urban landmarks support urban tourism by fascinating people and attracting tourists.

(Kei Ota)

Fig. 1 Tokyo Tower (photo by Kei Ota in January 2015)

Fig. 2 Tokyo Skytree (right) and adjacent commercial facility (left) (photo by Kei Ota in August 2012)

Mt. Takao: Tokyo's most popular mountain

●A world-class tourist destination

Mt. Takao located on the western edge of the extensive Kanto Plain is only an hour away from central Tokyo (Shinjuku Station) by train. It is a popular destination for school excursions in Tokyo and a day-hike not only for city dwellers but also for tourists from all over the country and the world (Fig. 1). More than 3 million people visit Mt. Takao annually and it is also known as "the most visited mountain in the world".

Why has Mt. Takao become an international tourist destination? Here we explore the reasons based on natural, historical and cultural perspectives.

●Rich natural environment of Mt. Takao

Mt. Takao, with an elevation of 599 m, is one of the peaks on the eastern edge of the Kanto Mountains. In the vicinity of Mt. Takao, there is an old stratum called the Kobotoke Group, which had been formed during Mesozoic Cretaceous period about 100 million years ago. Subsequent crustal movements have uplifted sand and mud deposited on the seabed, which resulted in the formation of Mt. Takao.

Mt. Takao boasts 1,598 species of plants. The natural forest of the mountain can be roughly divided into four categories based on the kinds of plants; Japanese red pine (coniferous trees), fir trees, oak (evergreen broad-leaved trees), and beech (deciduous broad-leaved trees) (Ref. 1). The ability to support both vegetation that is often found in cold northern Japan and vegetation that is relatively abundant in western Japan leads to the diversity of picturesque vegetation of Mt. Takao. The diversity of plants leads to the diversity of wildlife. Mt. Takao is known as a treasure trove of insects and also home to a large variety of wild birds and mammals.

Several political entities including the Tokugawa shogunate, imperial family and currently the government of Japan have extensively protected the natural environment of Mt. Takao. As a result, tourists visiting Mt. Takao can enjoy breathtaking "forest bathing", bird watching, and foliage "hunting". The existence of an unimaginably rich nature close to the urban center can be seen as the main reason behind the increasing popularity of Mt. Takao among the city dwellers and tourists.

●Mountain of faith and sightseeing

Mt. Takao is a mountain of faith. Yakuo-in temple on Mt. Takao belongs to the sacred Chizan school of Shingon sect, a major Buddhist school in Japan that practices Japanese mountain asceticism (*shugendo*).

Shugendo is a unique religion in Japan that tries to open up the path to enlightenment by carrying out rigorous training in the mountains, and those who practice *shugendo* are called *yamabushi* or *shugenja*, and wear unique costumes similar to forest goblins (*tengu*) in their daily trainings.

Ordinary people who started to visit the mountain during the Sengoku period of Japan are also known as the warring states period. The Hojo clan was dedicated to protect Mt. Takao as a place to pray for victory in the war. In the Edo period, faith in Mt. Fuji became popular, and many people wished to climb Mt. Fuji. Mt. Takao became an alternative pilgrimage for people who were unable to climb Mt. Fuji.

The opening of Keio electric track (current Keio Railway) and Kobu Railway (current JR

Chuo Line) significantly improved the access from central Tokyo and the number of climbers further increased in the Meiji and Showa eras. The Mt. Takao Cable Car started operating in 1927 and Mt. Takao became a prominent tourist destination in Japan where visitors can easily go for a day hike from central Tokyo.

●Michelin guide's three-star mountain

In 2007, Mt. Takao received three stars in the famous French travel guide book "Michelin Green Guide" (Ref. 2) as a place worth visiting, which triggered the interest in foreign travellers to explore the mountain. The number of foreigners has been increasing and Mt. Takao has evolved into a world-class tourist destination today.

As shown in Tab. 1, Michelin guide's three stars are mainly graded for the world heritage sites such as Mt. Fuji and prominent historical sites such as Kyoto and Nara. Mt. Takao has received a remarkable attention in the international guidebooks and it is even rated higher than famous Ginza and Asakusa in Tokyo.

Recently, many young women in Japan tend to enjoy climbing in fashionable outdoor clothes. These young women are called "*yama* (mountain) girls". Mt. Takao influences the fashion and leisure style of *yama* girls and can be identified as an impetus for the boom. (Akira Nakayama)

Fig. 1 Bustling entrance path of Mt. Takao (photo by Toshio Kikuchi in May 2019)

Tab. 1 Rating of Tourist destinations in the Michelin Green Guide (based on Ref. 2)

	★★★ worth a journey	★★ worth a detour	★ interesting
Tokyo	Shinjuku Gyoen National Garden	Roppongi Hills	Tokyo Tower
	Tokyo Metropolitan Government	Ginza	Shibuya
	Meiji Jingu	Tokyo Skytree	Odaiba
	Mt. Takao	Asakusa	Ueno Park
	Tokyo National Museum	Shinjuku	Harajuku
Around Tokyo	Nikko	Izu Islands	Yokohama
	Mt. Fuji	Miura Peninsula	Chuzenji Lake
	Kamakura	Shimoda	Hakone
		Jogasaki	Oyama
		Shuzenji	Kawaguchi Lake
Japan	Takayama	Osaka	Beppu
	Kyoto	Kanazawa	Kobe
	Nara	Ise-Shima	Uji
	Matsushima	Hiroshima	Sendai
	Shiretoko National Park	Matsumoto	Noto Peninsula

Ueno shopping streets and inbound tourism

●Location of the shopping streets

Ueno area in Tokyo is full of shopping opportunities and its shopping streets even appear
in international travel guidebooks. The
unique shopping street of "Ameyoko" has
become one of the main tourist attractions in
Ueno today. A variety of large and small
shopping streets are located within a radius
of approximately 300 m from JR Ueno Station and JR Okachimachi Station. The range
covers Showa-dori, Okachimachi-dori, the
area surrounded by Chuo-dori and the south
side of Ueno Park. Ueno shopping area
consists of eight shopping streets on the
east side of the JR rail track ("Ueno Ekimae
Ichibangai", "Ueno Station Main Street",
"Ueno Shoeikai", "Okachimachi Ekimae
Street", "Youth Road Ueno", "Ueno Okachimachi Chuo-dori", "Ueno U Road", and
"Ueno Sakura-dori") and nine on the west
side ("Ameyoko-dori Chuo", "Ameyoko
Odori", "Ueno Chuo", "Ameyoko Omote-
dori", "Ueno Naka-dori", "Okachimachi
Street", "Okachimachi Station South Exit",
"Ueno 2-chome Nakacho", and "Ikenohana
Nakacho") (Ref. 1).

●Store composition
Dining facilities
and fashion-related stores account for
38.6% of the business establishments in the
area. 27.6% of the business establishments are dining facilities such as cafeterias,
restaurants, grocery stores, and food and
beverage-related stores including bars (Ref.
2). There are about 161 fashion and acces-
sory stores such as cosmetics, jewelry and
clothing stores.

●Characteristics of the shopping streets

The number of stores or business establishments in each shopping street in Ueno is

mapped and summerized in Fig. 1. The
largest shopping street is "Ueno Okachimachi Chuo-dori" consisting 205 stores located
on the east side of the JR track. The second
largest shopping street is "Ueno Chuo-dori"
with 174 stores located on the west side of
the JR track. The third largest shopping
street is the "Ameyoko Omote-dori" with
143 stores.

The stores and establishments in these
three streets expand in the north-south direction. On the other hand, there are less
than 30 stores in the East-West direction
where "Ueno U Road", "Ueno Sakuradōri"
and "Okachimachi Station South Exit" shopping streets are located.

As summarized in Fig. 1, five types of
businesses could be identified; gifts, food
and beverage, management offices, factories, and others. A large ratio of the gift
stores could be found in "Ameyoko-dori
Central", "Ameyoko Omote-dori" and "Ueno
Okachimachi Chuo-dori" shopping streets.
The dining facilities such as restaurants are
concentrated around the JR Ueno Station
and in the south side of Ueno Park. Man-
agement-related offices such as education
and administration offices tend to increase
along the Chuo-dori and Showa-dori while
facilities that are not often used by tourists
such as factories can be found in "Ueno Station Main Street" and "Ueno Shoeikai" shopping streets located at a long distance from
the station.

●Increasing number of foreigners

With the recent increase in foreign tourists
nationwide, the number of foreigners visiting Ueno is also increasing.

Ameyoko, the most popular shopping

street in Ueno is featured in famous overseas travel guidebooks such as Lonely Planet and Time Out along with the other prominent tourist attractions such as the Tokyo National Museum and Ueno Zoo. The vibrant Asian shopping streets attract many foreign tourists. In particular, gift shops that sell Japanese souvenirs at reasonable prices get crowded with foreigners, especially tourists from Asian countries. At the same time, Middle-Eastern style kebab stores are increasing in Ameyoko and some mosques and prayer facilities are also created around Okachimachi Station reflecting the increase of Muslim visitors and residents in Ueno (Fig. 3).

(Kei Ota)

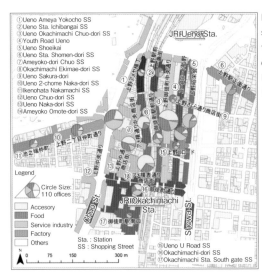

Fig. 1 Characteristics of shopping streets in the Ueno area (based on facility data with Zenrin's locational data provided by the Center for Spatial Information Science (CSIS), the University of Tokyo (Study No. 268)

Fig. 2 The bustling Ameyoko and Kaminaka shopping streets (photo by Kei Ota in March 2016)

Fig. 3 A building converted into a mosque (photo by Kei Ota in March 2019)

Conclusion Tokyo's Future: Sustainable Tokyo

Tokyo Station, the origin point of Japan's railway transportation (photo by Toshio Kikuchi in May 2019)

Tokyo has developed as the capital city of Japan and also as a leading global city where people, goods, capital and information are concentrated. On the other hand, Tokyo strives for coexistence of urban and rural spaces and simultaneously focuses on the enhancement of amenities in its urban and residential environments while overcoming repeated disasters.

1   Tokyo as a primate city

Japan's land area is divided into several regions, and each region is managed and governed by the central cities such as Sendai, Nagoya and Hiroshima. It is common to carry out these operations by establishing regional administrative offices and corporate branches. For example, there are nine Regional Transport Bureaus under the administrative jurisdiction of Ministry of Land, Infrastructure, Transport and Tourism (Hokkaido, Tohoku, Kanto, Hokuriku-Shinetsu, Chubu, Kinki (including the Kobe Transport Management Department), Chugoku, Shikoku, Kyushu Transport Bureaus (including Okinawa General Bureau for Okinawa Prefecture)). The territorial jurisdiction of the Regional Transportation Bureaus is set considering the prefectures as the basic administrative unit and several other factors including the proximity to a regional central city based on topographic and road conditions, and possibility of easy maintenance and management of road traffic. The Ministry of Land, Infrastructure, Transport and Tourism, the authority that oversees and manages the Regional Transport Bureaus is located in Tokyo forming a hierarchical structure where Tokyo presides over the regional central cities or the center that controls the regions. In other words, a dominant-dominated type of urban system centered on the capital city of Tokyo is formed (Ref. 1).

Similar hierarchical structure can be found in headquarter-branch relationships and administration spheres of information and communication sectors of many companies and banks (Fig. 1). As an example of an operation related to information dissemination, the Japan Broadcasting Corporation (Nippon Hoso Kyokai, NHK)'s administration sphere of regional broadcasting stations is divided into eight areas as Hokkaido, Tohoku, Kanto/Koshinetsu, Tokai/Hokuriku, Kansai, Chugoku, Shikoku, and Kyushu/Okinawa areas (Fig. 1). Jurisdiction of each broadcasting station covers news, projects, and weather forecasts that are relevant to the local situations, and NHK's regional divisions have become an important base for disseminating original local information. A main characteristic of these regional divisions is that it considers the regional classification of natural features mainly related to climate and weather in order to provide information on regional weather forecasts. Early transmission of information on the local society, economy, and current events is also an important role of a public broadcast. Therefore, the regional divisions are set based not only on social and economic considerations, but also on regional cohesion of culture. For example, the Kanto and Koushinetsu areas operate as a single unit, considering the level of commuting and logistics centering on Tokyo, and the movement of people for leisure and sightseeing. Further, broadcasts of national news, weather, and other information are carried out from the studios in Tokyo. In other words, while there is an emphasis on region based broadcasts, national information is transmitted from Tokyo in a unified manner forming a hierarchical network of information centered on Tokyo.

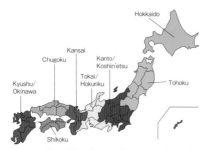

Fig. 1 Classification of areas by the broadcasting stations of the Japan Broadcasting Corporation (NHK) (based on Ref. 2)

Fig. 2 Tokyo's Marunouchi district, where head office functions are concentrated (photo by Toshio Kikuchi in November 2013)

As described above, the centrality of Tokyo as a city today is clearly evident with its concentration of people, goods, capital (money) and information. The unipolar concentration and high centrality of Tokyo displays the characteristics of a primate city (Fig. 2). However, it has also led to several issues such as regional disparities between the center (Tokyo) and the periphery, and deterioration of the urban environment. Modern Tokyo is challenged with all the common environmental, social, and economic problems facing the other megacities in the world, and resolving these problems is an important role of Tokyo as a global city (Ref. 3).

2 Enhancing and expanding the centrality of Tokyo

After World War II, Tokyo has become a place where people, goods, capital (money) and information are concentrated, ensuring its position as a global city. According to the UN's World Urbanization Prospects, Tokyo has the world's largest urban population of about 37 million in 2010. As shown in the world air route map in Fig. 3, along with Hong Kong, Dubai, Los Angeles, London and Paris, Tokyo is a huge nodal city where various air routes are concentrated, and it is also a global city where many people gather from all over the world. However, simply gathering a large number of people does not make Tokyo a global city. Collecting goods, information and capital (money) together with

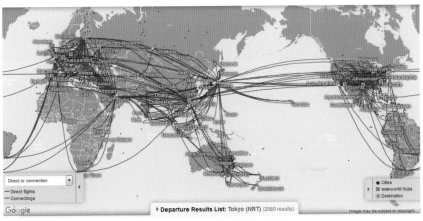

Fig. 3　World air route map (Ref. 4)

Air routes of the Oneworld from the New Tokyo International Air Port at Narita. The red line is a direct service, and the blue line is an indirect sevice.

people is important in becoming a global city (Ref. 5).

According to Fig. 4, which shows the number of patent applications by cities worldwide (2003-2005), Tokyo has more patent applications related to information and communications than Silicon Valley and represents a prominent presence among the other global cities in the world.　With a relatively large number of patent applications even in other fields, Tokyo is a hub of information on various technological innovations.　Therefore, Tokyo can be considered a global city where people, goods, capital (money) and information gather, and centrality excels.　Even though, Tokyo can enjoy a new civilization of the 21st century under such circumstances, it stands at a major crossroad in choosing its path for future, which requires the shape and character of a megacity that adapts to the borderless era in which people, capital (money), information, and goods are on an unprecedented scale moving at low cost and instantaneously to specific bases and nodes.

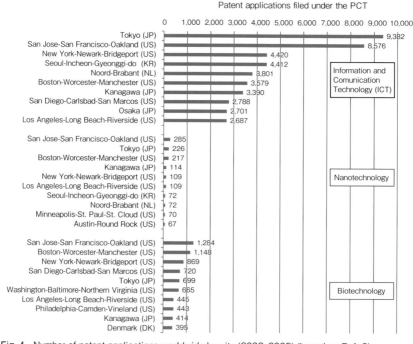

Fig. 4　Number of patent applications worldwide by city (2003-2005) (based on Ref. 6)
Top regions by the number of international patent applications in the fields of information technology, nanotechnology and biotechnology.

3 Realizing a symbiotic city

One of the major characteristics of the global city of Tokyo is that it is striving to solve the problems associated with the urban and living environments that mega cities have in common, by coexisting with natural and agricultural spaces. Natural spaces such as forests and green spaces in Tokyo have decreased due to the expansion of urban land use during the period of high economic growth. However, since the 1990s, the remaining forests in Tokyo have been properly managed, and new green spaces have been created ensuring Tokyo's progress as a global city aiming to coexist with nature. Originally, the rural forests of Musashino Uplands spread in the western suburbs of Tokyo, and abundant natural resources of water protection forests remained in the Okutama area. At the same time, the Ogasawara Islands float in the Pacific Ocean, about 1,000 km away from the center of Tokyo, where Tokyo's proud world natural heritage site is found. Such natural environments of Tokyo are changing from being developed to being conserved and protected, and are also being targeted for appropriate usage and enhancement of amenities.

For example, the Musashino Uplands developed as reclamation land during the Edo period creating an image of a natural and rural space with expanse of forests and farmlands. After World War II, with the expansion of residential areas into the suburbs, the forests and agricultural lands in Musashino were converted to urban land use, and nature was lost causing a deterioration of urban residential environment. Tokyo realized the importance of improving the quality and amenities of the living environment, and being considerate of the global environment. Necessary initiatives were taken to create a city that can exist in harmony with surrounding nature, such as forests and *satoyama* (rural forests). For example, a greenway was developed along the Tamagawa Josui Waterworks, which was excavated in the Edo period, and a part of the Musashino forest has been preserved and well managed (Fig. 5). The Tamagawa Josui Waterworks' greenway not only provides an amenity to the urban living environment, but also provides urban residents with a leisure space for walking and jogging. Hence, Tokyo aims to become a global city that coexists with nature in order to secure and sustain a good living environment and healthy lifestyles for its urban residents (Ref. 7).

In order to support the large population of Tokyo, coexistence with agricultural space is also considered very important. Historically, Tokyo has worked in

Fig. 5 Tamagawa Josui Waterworks flowing through the Musashino Uplands and its greenway (photo by Toshio Kikuchi in June 2007)

Fig. 6 Urban agriculture and farmer's direct sale booth in Kodaira city in the western suburbs of Tokyo (photo by Toshio Kikuchi in June 2011)

various ways to feed its huge population. The development of suburban farming and transport infrastructure for food supply has played an important role in balancing food demand and supply in Tokyo. Various production areas in Japan supply food for the Tokyo Market, and the sources of food supply continued to expand. As a result, overseas production areas also started to supply food for Tokyo, triggering the globalization of food supply. Such changes in the food system are based on the economic gain approach and "economy of scale", and consumers sought for a large quantity of cheap, uniform and standardized food.

In the 21st century, the production, supply, and consumption of food did not require economic profits or efficiencies, but rather added value. Such added value has not only led to the upgrading and branding of food production, but also to several changes in food supply such as supply of fresh, safe and secure food through direct food sales at farms. In Tokyo, the agricultural space is maintained as urban farming, and fresh, safe and secure food cultivated in these agricultural spaces is directly supplied to urban residents through farmers' direct sales (Fig. 6). Farmers' direct sales booths serve not only as a place to provide food to urban residents, but also as a link between the urban communities and the local rural communities, helping to sustain the conservation of agricultural spaces. Tokyo seeks to achieve better food and lifestyles and social sustainability such as community support by coexisting with agricultural spaces.

4 Tokyo as a disaster-mitigation city and disaster-conquering city

Fighting disasters and recovering from disasters have been a part of the

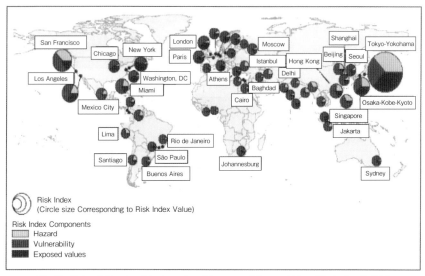

Fig. 7 Natural disaster risks in major cities around the world (modified after Ref. 9)

history of Edo and Tokyo. Creating a disaster resilient city has become a vital issue in the global city of Tokyo. Fig. 7 shows the distribution of natural disaster risks in various cities around the world as surveyed by foreign insurance companies, and it is clear that Tokyo has a much higher risk of natural disasters than any other cities in the world. In particular, the underlying causes of disasters are multiple, and are closely related to the fact that Japan's territory is located in the interplate zone and typhoon routes that occur over the Pacific Ocean. Furthermore, the number of actual disasters was relatively high, which seemed a major obstacle for Tokyo to develop into a megacity or global city. On the other hand, in terms of physical and social vulnerability, the overall proportion of the risks was lower than the other cities around the world. This suggests that, in consideration of the risks of natural disasters, Tokyo is proceeding with the hard measures to reduce damage to the buildings and infrastructure, and also with soft measures of disaster mitigation such as evacuation and preparedness of residents (Ref. 8).

Based on the lessons learned from repeated disasters, Edo and Tokyo have incorporated various disaster prevention efforts into urban development, and the global city of Tokyo is currently sending many messages to the world, not as a disaster-prevention city but as a disaster-mitigation city or a disaster-controlling city. Nogawa River and its basin are examples of landscapes that symbolize a disaster mitigation and controlling city (Fig. 8). Nogawa River is one of the urban rivers, and empties into the Tama River. Urban rivers receive rainfall directly as surface flow due to the concrete and asphalt land cover in the basin. As a result, many urban

Fig. 8 Nogawa River flowing through an urban area in the western suburbs of Tokyo (photo by Toshio Kikuchi in November 2013)

rivers are more likely to cause urban floods during typhoons and guerilla torrential rain (localized torrential rain). As a hard measure to prevent urban flood disasters, construction work has been carried out under disaster prevention projects to straighten the flow of urban rivers and build concrete embankments of both riverbanks and riverbed.

However, these disaster prevention works destroy ecosystems and significantly reduce the biodiversity of rivers. Nogawa River preserves its ecosystem and biodiversity by keeping natural slopes without encasing the riverbanks and riverbed in concrete while retaining natural river flows as much as possible. The preserved nature has also become leisure space for urban residents. Although the city is exposed to the threat of urban floods as a price for preserving nature, the Nogawa River has a retarding pond that has been designed to reduce disasters. Disaster prevention is important, however, there are practical issues and disasters can lead to a loss of valuable nature and landscapes, and impair the amenities of urban environment. Consequently, instead of preventing disasters, the idea of mitigating and overcoming disasters has spread in the global city of Tokyo. (Toshio Kikuchi)

Afterword

Tokyo is undoubtedly a global city. Its journey as a global city began in the mid Edo period, and has continued to the present day over a period of 300 years. How did Tokyo sustain its journey as a global city to this day? Even though, both Edo and Tokyo were catastrophic due to fires, earthquakes and war, the city has been able to revive from each disaster and evolve with extremely enhanced power. How did Edo and Tokyo continue to flourish? How did Edo and Tokyo managed to grow exceptionally regardless of repeated disasters? The motivation for planning this book was to explore these secrets of Edo and Tokyo. Fortunately, Tokyo Metropolitan University and its Department of Geography have been conducting area studies on Tokyo from various aspects including physical geography and human geography. We believed that making use of these accumulated research findings would help to figure out the answers to the questions that provoked the idea of this book. Accordingly, the graduates and academic staff of Tokyo Metropolitan University and its Department of Geography worked on writing this book.

The book takes various approaches to unravel the secrets of Tokyo and discover the driving forces of its development. The driving forces may have evolved from the contrasting and harmonious nature of Tokyo's contradictory characteristics. To be specific, Tokyo is rich in nature, despite being a man-made metropolis. In other words, Tokyo has evolved based on the contrast and harmony between artifacts and nature. Similar contrast and harmony are applicable for the situations of "new and old", "innovation and tradition", "sacred and profane", "ordinary and celebrity", "quiet and congested", "individuals and masses" and "usual and unusual". These contrasts are reflected in the current state of Tokyo, and the harmony of those contrasts is the attraction of Tokyo, making it a mysterious global city. This book aims to pursue the charms and wonders of Tokyo and if you read this book and rediscover Tokyo, it will be an utmost delight for each author.

Above all, what kind of place is Tokyo for you? Before you understand the charms and wonders, there could also be doubts on the livability of Tokyo. It is difficult to say whether it is easy or hard to live in Tokyo, but according to the foreigners that I know, Tokyo is one of the most livable cities in the world. The main reasons include the stability of political economy and sustainability of social security. Canadian urban geographer, Prof. Sorensen wrote in his book "The Making of Urban Japan", "Edo is the city that I find most attractive in the 19th century. Edo is a compact city despite being a mega city, and above all an eco-city". Tokyo's livability and convenience are supported by its compactness-based town planning and traditions of town planning focused on living in harmony with nature and agricultural space. Through this book, we also hope to disseminate an understanding about the various aspects of Tokyo's livability to everyone. This book was originally published in Japanese and the current English edition includes the same contents. We hope the English edition will enable many foreigners to understand not only the charm and wonders of Tokyo, but also the convenience of living in Tokyo more than the Japanese.

The Japanese name of the Tokyo Metropolitan University changed from "Toritsu Daigaku" to "Shuto Daigaku Tokyo" and again to the original name of "Toritsu Daigaku" at present. Tokyo Metropolitan University's Department of Geography moved from Meguro Ward to Minami-Osawa in Hachioji City and the Faculty of Science changed to the Faculty of Urban Environmental Sciences. At the same time, the Department of Tourism Science was newly established in the new faculty in connection with the Department of Geography. The transition of the Department of Geography is dramatic, however, its stance for clarifying Tokyo's area, places and spaces from various viewpoints and being the frontier of research remains unchanged.

Lastly, I would like to thank the Editorial Department of Asakura Publishing Co., Ltd. for taking care of everything from planning to editing in publishing this book.

April 2020
On behalf of the authors at the Minami-Osawa Campus
Toshio Kikuchi

Glossary　（*: period/era name）

Ansei* （安政）　A Japanese era name. 1855-1860.

cho （町）　town

-chome （丁目）　district.

class A river, class B river, class C river （一級河川，二級河川，三級河川）　Japanese public river classification based on the importance for flood control and economy.

-dori （通り）　street

Edo （江戸）　The former name of Tokyo.

Edo castle （江戸城）　The castle of shoguns of Tokugawa shogunate.

Edo period* （江戸時代）　A historic period from the foundation of the Tokugawa shogunate (1603) to the beginning of Meiji era (1868).

fudo （不動）　A kind of Buddhist temples, originated from the worship for the Buddhist deity Fudo Myoo （不動明王），or Acala in Sanscrit name.

Genroku* （元禄）　A Japanese era name. 1688-1704.

Goto Shimpei （後藤新平，1857-1929）　A Japanese politician in Meiji and Taisho eras and the seventh mayor of Tokyo City.

guerilla torrential rain （ゲリラ豪雨）　Japanese expression of local heavy rain in a short time.

Gyoen （御苑）　parks with its origin of garden of Emperor，such as the Shinjuku Gyoen and the Gyoen in Meiji Jingu (see p.51-52)

-hashi (bashi) （橋）　bridge.

Heisei* （平成）　A Japanese era name. 1989-2019.

Hoei* （宝永）　A Japanese era name. 1709-1735.

-ji （寺）　Buddhist temple.

Jogan* （貞観）　A Japanese era name. 876-884.

kabayaki （蒲焼き）　Japanese traditional food preparation of fish, especially eel grilled with a sauce made from eel stock, soy sayce, sweet rice wine and sugar.

kaiseki （懐石）　traditional multi-course meal served before a tea-ceremony.

Kanto （関東）　An area in Japan including Tokyo Metropolis, Saitama, Chiba, Kanagawa, Gunma, Tochigi, and Ibaraki Prefectures.

-kawa (gawa) （川）　river

Kawabata Yasunari （川端康成）　A Japanese novelist and the first Japanese laureate of the Nobel Prize in Literature.

Kuroshio （黒潮）　A ocean current in the Pacific Ocean, flowing to the north through the south of Japanese archipelago.

Kyoto （京都）　A city in Kansai area. The palace of Emperor was located in Kyoto until the Meiji era.

-machi （町）　town

Masaoka Shiki （正岡子規）　A Japanese haiku poet in Meiji era.

Matsumoto Reiji （松本零士，1938-）　A Japanese manga animator well known for his work "Galaxy Express 999" and others.

Meiji* （明治）　A Japanese era name. 1868-1912.

mirin （みりん）　sweet rice wine

Mito （水戸）　Prefectural capital of Ibaraki Prefecture.

mon（文） Japanese traditional currency used until the early Meiji era. 4000 mon is 1 gold ryo （両）. According to modern monetary value, 1 mon is about 32 yen.

Mt. Fuji (Fuji-san)（富士山） The highest mountain in Japan, with 3,776 m elavation, located at the boader of Shizuoka and Yamanashi Prefectures.

Nagasaki（長崎） A port city in the Kyushu area. In Edo period Nagasaki was the only port in Japan open to the other countries.

NHK Nippon Hoso Kyokai. The official English name is Japan Broadcasting Corporation.

Ota Dokan（太田道灌, 1432-1486） A Japanese samurai and Buddhist monk in 15th cencury, also known as the architect of Edo castle.

prefectures（都道府県, todofuken） Japanese administrative subdivision. Japan is divided into 47 prefectures; Tokyo Metropolis（東京都）, Hokkaido prefecture（北海道）, Osaka Prefecture（大阪府）, Kyoto Prefecture（京都府）, and other 43 Prefectures（県）.

Sagami Bay（相模湾） Marine area that simultaneously faces to Kanagawa and Shizuoka Prefectures

samurai（侍） a Japanese warrior.

-san (zan)（山） mountain

sen（銭） Japanese currency. Sen has the same value as mon in Edo period.

Seven Lucky Gods Pilgrimage（七福神） The seven deities of good luck and happiness; Benzaiten（弁財天）, Daikokuten（大黒天）, Jurojin（寿老人）, Bishamonten（毘沙門天）, Hotei（布袋）, Ebisu（恵比寿）, and Fukurokuju（福禄寿）. Each of them has its origin in Indian, Chinese, or Japanese culture.

Shibusawa Eiichi（渋沢栄一, 1840-1930） A Japanese industrialist in Meiji, Taisho, and Showa eras, and the founder of the First National Bank（第一国立銀行） in Japan.

-shima/jima（島） island

shogun（将軍） The title of hereditary leader of Japan.

Showa*（昭和） A Japanese era name. 1926-1989.

special ward（特別区） A special municipalities in Japan. The central area of Tokyo Metropolis is divided into 23 special wards.

sub-centers（副都心） New city centers in Tokyo, such as Shibuya, Shinjuku, and Ikebukuro.

sugoroku（双六） Japanese board game played with dice.

Sunpu（駿府） the former name of Shizuoka city.

Taisho*（大正） A Japanese era name. 1912-1926.

Tama（多摩） The west area of Tokyo Metropolis.

Tamagawa brothers（玉川兄弟） The architects of the Tamagawa Josui waterworks in Edo period: Shoemon and Seiemon.

Tenkai（天海, 1536-1643） A Buddhist monk in early Edo period. He served as a consultant to first three shoguns.

tofu（豆腐） Japanese food made of coagulating soy milk.

Tokugawa Ieyasu（徳川家康, 1543-1616） The founder of the Tokugawa shogunate.

ukiyo-e（浮世絵） A genre of Japanese art, in forms of woodblock prints and paintings, depicting the lives of people in Edo period.

Uraga（浦賀） A area in Yokosuka city. In 1853 The first expedition ships of United Stetes visited Uraga and forced Tokugawa Shogunate to open Japan ports.

-yama（山） mountain

References

Introduction: Discover Tokyo
1) Japan Map Center, 2013. Map: Paper maps of the Geospatial Information Authority of Japan. [http://www.jmc.or.jp/buy_map_kami.html] (last accessed 21 March 2019) (in Japanese)
2) Kanno, M., Sano, M. and Taniuchi, T., 2009. Regional geography of Japan, vol. 5, Greater Tokyo Area. Asakura Publishing. (in Japanese)
3) Tokyo Metropolis, 2018. Population/area by wards, cities, towns, villages. [http://www.metro.tokyo.jp/tosei/tokyoto/profile/gaiyo/kushichoson.html] (last accessed 28 January 2019) (in Japanese)
4) Bureau of Statistics, Ministry of Internal Affairs and Communications, 2019. National census in 2015. [http://www.stat.go.jp/data/kokusei/2015/] (last accessed 20 January 2019) (in Japanese)
5) Okuma, T., 1981. Changes in flood controls and flood damages of Tone River. University of Tokyo Press. (in Japanese)
6) Geospatial Information Authority of Japan, 2006. Digital elevation map of Kanto, Tokyo Metropolis (document D1-No.455). [http://www.gsi.go.jp/kankyochiri/degitalelevationmap_kanto.html] (last accessed 21 March 2019) (in Japanese)
7) Kaizuka, S., 1979. Natural history of Tokyo, second edition. Kinokuniya Company. (in Japanese)
8) Japanese Paleolithic Society, 2019: Paleolithic sites in the Japanese archipelago. [http://palaeolithic.jp/sites/index.html] (last accessed 21 March 2019) (in Japanese)
9) Kaizuka, S., Koike, K., Endo, K., Yamazaki, H. and Suzuki, T., (eds.) 2000: Regional geomorphology of the Japanese Islands, vol.4, Geomorphology of Kanto and Izu-Ogasawara. University of Tokyo Press. (in Japanese)

Chapter 1: Tokyo's Landforms
1) Kaizuka, S., Koike, K., Endo, K., Yamazaki, H. and Suzuki T., 2000. Regional geomorphology of the Japanese Islands, vol. 4, Geomorphology of Kanto and Izu-Ogasawara. University of Tokyo Press. (in Japanese)
2) Yonekura, N., Kaizuka, S., Nogami, M. and Chinzei, K., 2001. Regional geomorphology of the Japanese Islands, vol. 1, Introduction to Japanese geomorphology. University of Tokyo Press. (in Japanese)
3) Japanese Geological Society (eds.), 2008. Monograph on geology of Japan, Vol.3, Kanto. Asakura Publishing. (in Japanese)

Close-up: Kanda River and its flow
1) Matsumoto, Y., 2009. Kanda River. In Takahashi, Y. (ed.) Encyclopedia of rivers. 264, Maruzen. (in Japanese)
2) Matsumoto, Y., 2013. Kanda River. In Takahashi, Y., Takara, K., Nonomura, K. and Haruyama, S. (eds.) Encyclopedia of the world's rivers. 184-185, Maruzen. (in Japanese)
3) Iwaya, T., 2013. Rivers under the ring road no. 7. In Takahashi, Y., Takara, K., Nonomura, K. and Haruyama, S. (eds.) Encyclopedia of the world's rivers. 185, Maruzen. (in Japanese)

Close-up: Tokyo's underground
1) Commission for the Consideration of Tokyo's Directly Underground Earthquake, Cabinet Office, 2013. Report on Tokyo M7 class earthquake, Sagami trough M8 class earthquake epicenter fault model and magnitude distribution, tsunami height (maps). [http://www.bousai.go.jp/kaigirep/chuobou/senmon/shutochokkajishinmodel/pdf/dansoumodel_02.pdf] (last accessed 2 April 2019) (in Japanese)

Close-up: Earthquakes and countermeasures
1) Central Disaster Prevention Committee for the Direct Earthquake Working Group, The Government of Japan, 2013. Predictions regarding the direct earthquake under Tokyo and

measures (Newest edition) [http://www.bousai.go.jp/jishin/syuto/taisaku_wg/pdf/syuto_wg_report.pdf].

2) Bureau of Urban Development, Tokyo Metropolitan Government, "Your Community's Earthquake Risk 2018" [https://www.toshiseibi.metro.tokyo.lg.jp/bosai/chousa_6/download/earthquake_risk.pdf] (last accessed 30 January 2020)

Close-up: Mt. Fuji and Tokyo

1) Suzuki, T., 2013. The history and future of volcanic disaster in Tokyo and the surrounding areas. Journal of Geography (Chigaku Zasshi), 122, 1088-1098. Tokyo Geological Society. (in Japanese)

Chapter 2: Tokyo's Climate

1) Takahashi, H., Shimizu, S., Yamato, H., Seto, Y. and Yokoyama, H., 2014. Wintertime nocturnal temperature distribution based on spatially high density observation data in the Tokyo Metropolitan area under clear sky and weak wind conditions. Journal of Geography (Chigaku Zasshi) 123, 189-210. (in Japanese)

2) Yamato, H., Mikami. T. and Takahashi, H., 2017. Impact of sea breeze penetration over urban areas on midsummer temperature distributions in the Tokyo Metropolitan area. International Journal of Climatology 37, 5154-5169.

3) Seto, Y., Fukushima, A. and Takahashi, H., 2019. Regional distribution of the transition time of local wind systems in summer in the south Kanto region. E-journal GEO 14, 223-232. (in Japanese)

4) Takahashi, K. and Takahashi, H., 2013. Influence of urban heat island phenomenon in the central Tokyo on nocturnal local wind system in summer: A case study using atmospheric pressure data of high density observation network. Tenki 60, 505-519. (in Japanese)

5) Harada, A., 1981. An analytical study of nocturnal low-level jet over Kanto plain, Japan. Papers in Meteorology and Geophysics 32, 233-245.

Close-up: Why summer in Tokyo is not only "hot" but also "humid"?

1) Takahashi, H.G., Adachi, S. A., Sato, T., Hara, M., Ma, X. and Kimura, F., 2015. An oceanic impact of the Kuroshio on surface air temperature on the Pacific coast of Japan in summer: Regional H_2O greenhouse gas effect. Journal of Climate 28, 7128-7144.

Close-up: "Guerilla" torrential rains

1) Shepherd, J. M., Pierce, H. and Negri, J. A., 2002. Rainfall modification by major urban areas: Observation from spaceborne rain radar on the TRMM satellite. Journal of Applied Meteorology 41, 689-701.

2) Takahashi, H., 2010. The city and precipitation phenomena. In Fukuoka, Y. and Nakagawa, K. (eds.) Why are inland cities hot? From Kumagaya, the hottest city in Japan. Seizando Shoten, 75-102. (in Japanese)

3) Takahashi, H., Nakamura, Y. and Suzuki, H. 2011. Frequency distribution of intense rainfall in the wards of Tokyo and its relationship with the spatial structure of building heights. Journal of Geography (Chigaku Zasshi) 120, 359-381. (in Japanese)

Chapter 3: Vegetation and Wildlife in Tokyo

1) Shimano, K. and Nakatsu, S., 1993. Regeneration of mixed *Fagus crenata-Fagus japonica* forests in Mt. Mito, Okutama, west of Tokyo. Japanese Journal of Ecology 43, 13-19. (in Japanese)

2) Fukushima, T., 2017. Walks in Tokyo's forests: color version. Kodansha. (in Japanese)

3) Tokyo Metropolitan University Ogasawara Project 2003, 2004. Ogasawara's culture and nature: aiming at co-existence of people and nature. Tokyo Metropolitan University. (in Japanese)

4) Ueda, M. and Sato, N., 2018. Changes in Tokyo's birds since the 1970s. Bird Research News (1 January 2018). [http://db3.bird-research.jp/news/201801-no1/] (last accessed 28 February 2019) (in Japanese)

5) Hamura City History Editorial Committee, 2019. Hamura City's historical records, Nature. Hamura City. (in Japanese)

6) Tokyo Metropolis, 2017. The 5th plan for the management of sika deer in Tokyo. [http://www.

metro.tokyo.jp/tosei/hodohappyo/press/2017/03/30/documents/25_02.pdf] (last accessed 28 February 2019). (in Japanese)

7) Kato, K., 2003. Faunal change of stream fishes in the Tama River and Tokyo Metropolitan area, due to economical development of watershed. Aquabiology 25, 123-130. (in Japanese)

8) Yoshikawa, M., 2017. Grasses in the floodplain. In Fukushima T. (ed.), Compendium of Japanese vegetation, 2nd edition. Asakura Publishing, 152-153. (in Japanese)

9) Natural Environment Division, Bureau of Environment, Tokyo Metropolitan Government (ed.), 2010. 2010 Red list of threatened species in Tokyo: 23 ward and Tama area version. Natural Environment Division, Bureau of Environment, Tokyo Metropolitan Government. (in Japanese)

10) National Institute for Environmental Studies 2019: Invasive species data base [https://www.nies. go.jp/biodiversity/invasive/index.html] (last accessed 28 February 2019). (in Japanese)

11) Inoue, D. and Ishii, M. (eds.), 2016. Distribution of butterflies. Hokuryukan. (in Japanese)

Jingu's forest

1) Meiji Jingu Office, 1980. Report on the results of the comprehensive survey on the environment of Meiji Shrine. (in Japanese)

2) Okutomi, K., Matsuzaki, Y. and Ikeda, H., 2013. Forest vegetation of Meiji Jingu (Results of the second comprehensive survey of the environment of Meiji Shrine, on the 100th anniversary of its creation). Meiji Jingu Office. (in Japanese)

3) Fukushima, T. (ed.), 2017. Illustrated Japanese vegetation (second edition). Asakura Publishing. (in Japanese)

Close-up: *Satoyama*

1) Forestry Agency (ed.), 1958. Summary of forestry statistics. Forestry Public Association. (in Japanese)

2) Ogura, J., 2005. Human activities and vegetation. Landscape Ecology and Management 9, 3-11. (in Japanese)

3) Miyawaki, A. (ed.), 1975. Ecological survey on environmental conservation in the western area of the Tama New Town. Yokohama National University Press. (in Japanese)

4) Miyawaki, A. (ed.), 1986. Vegetation of Japan, vol. 7 Kanto. Shibundo. (in Japanese)

5) National Institute for Environmental Studies NIES, 2019. Invasive species data base [https://www. nies.go.jp/biodiversity/invasive/index.html] (last accessed 28 February 2019) (in Japanese)

Close-up: Tokyo's raccoon dogs

1) Takaoka, S., 2013. Urbanization and faunal changes over the past 100 years in and around Tokyo Metropolis. Journal of Geography (Chigaku Zasshi) 122, 1020-1038. (in Japanese)

2) Miyamoto, T., Shioya, T. and NPO Urban Wild-Life Institute, 2008. The surprising life of Tokyo's raccoon dogs—coexistence of wildlife in the metropolis. Geijutsu Hyoron. (in Japanese)

3) Masuda, R., 2017. Raccoon dogs on the Imperial Palace grounds. Biogeography of mammals. University of Tokyo Press. 126-133. (in Japanese)

4) Takatsuki, S., 2017. Food habits of the raccoon dog at the Tsuda University's Kodaira Campus, western Tokyo. Humans and Nature 28, 1-10. (in Japanese)

5) Yamamoto, Y. and Kinoshita, A., 1994. Food composition of raccoon dogs *Nyctereutes procyonoides viverrinus* in Kawasaki. Bulletin of the Kawasaki Municipal Science Museum 5, 29-34. (in Japanese)

Chapter 4: Tokyo's Waters and Seas

1) Bureau of Construction, Tokyo Metropolitan Government, 2018. Management and utilization of rivers. [http://www.kensetsu.metro.tokyo.jp/kasen/gaiyo/02.html] (last accessed 27 December 2018) (in Japanese)

2) Bureau of Environment, Tokyo Metropolitan Government, 2018. Springs in Tokyo: Map of springs. Bureau of Environment, Tokyo Metropolitan Government. (in Japanese)

3) Izumi, K., 2004. The origin of modern water resource conservation forests: An ecological history of forests and cities. University of Tokyo Press. (in Japanese)

4) Ministry of the Environment, Government of Japan, 2018. Annual report on the environment, the sound material-cycle society, and the biodiversity in Japan. [http://www.env.go.jp/policy/hakusyo/] (last accessed 27 December 2018) (in Japanese)

5) Japan Coast Guard, 2018. Information on sea area under Japanese jurisdiction: Territorial sea of Japan. [https://www1.kaiho.mlit.go.jp/JODC/ryokai/ryokai_setsuzoku.html] (last accessed 27 December 2018) (in Japanese)

6) Hydrographic and Oceanographic Department, Japan Coast Guard, 2018. Terminologies related to the territorial sea of Japan. [http://www1.kaiho.mlit.go.jp/JODC/ryokai/zyoho/msk_idx.html] (last accessed 27 December 2018) (in Japanese)

7) Ministry of Foreign Affairs of Japan, 2018. Extended continental shelf and initiatives by Japan. [https://www.mofa.go.jp/mofaj/press/pr/wakaru/topics/vol172/index.html] (last accessed 27 December 2018) (in Japanese)

8) Yamada, Y., 2010. Japan is 4th marine empire of the world. Kodansha. (in Japanese)

9) Ministry of Economy, Trade and Industry, Japan, 2018. Rare earth metals. [http://www.meti.go.jp/policy/nonferrous_metal/rareearth/rareearth.html] (last accessed 27 December 2018) (in Japanese)

10) The Yomiuri Shimbun Tokyo Head Office, 2019. Toward rich deep sea conservation area. Evening edition of Yomiuri Shimbun issued by Tokyo Head Office on 18th January, 2019. (in Japanese)

11) Ministry of Agriculture, Forestry and Fisheries, Japan, 2018. The rate for fish calorie self-sufficiency in Japan. [http://www.jfa.maff.go.jp/j/kikaku/wpaper/h23_h/trend/1/t1_2_1_4.html.] (last accessed 27 December 2018) (in Japanese)

Close-up: Water buses on Sumida River

1) Tanaka, S., 1988. Water buses and Sumida River. Shin-toshi 42, 85-88. (in Japanese)

2) Ota, K., 2014. A study on the transition of water bus routes and ship diversification in the Tokyo Waterfront Area. The International Journal of Tourism Science 7, 37-44. (in Japanese)

Close-up: Natural springs and *tōfu* production

1) Bureau of Environment, Tokyo Metropolitan Government, 2018. Springs in Tokyo: Map of springs. Bureau of Environment, Tokyo Metropolitan Government. (in Japanese)

2) Hayakawa, H. 1992, Natural water in Tokyo, new edition. Rural Culture Association Japan. (in Japanese)

Close-up: Edo's waterworks

1) Watabe, K., 2004. Musashino's waterworks.Tokai University Press. (in Japanese)

Close-up: Tokyo's hot springs

1) Ministry of the Environment, 2014. Guidelines for analyzing mineral springs (revised version in 2014). [http://www.env.go.jp/council/12nature/y123-14/mat04.pdf] (last accessed 27 November 2018) (in Japanese)

2) Kimbara, K., 1992. Distribution map and catalogue of hot and mineral springs in Japan. Geological Survey of Japan. (in Japanese)

3) The Yomiuri Shimbun Tokyo Head Office, 2018a. Why are black hot springs mainly originated in Tokyo Metropolis? Morning Edition of Yomiuri Shimbun Issued by Tokyo Head Office on 8th October, 2018. (in Japanese)

4) The Yomiuri Shimbun Tokyo Head Office, 2018b. Learning invention for activating hot spring baths. Morning Edition of Yomiuri Shimbun Issued by Tokyo Head Office on 21 October, 2018. (in Japanese)

Chapter 5: Tokyo's History and Culture

1) Takahashi, Y., Yoshida, N., Miyamoto, M. and Ito, T., 1993. Atlas on the history of Japanese cities. University of Tokyo Press. (in Japanese)

2) Screech, T., translation by Morishita, M., 2007. The great building of Edo: poetics and planning in the Tokugawa metropolis. Kodansha. (in Japanese)

3) Miyamoto, K., 1996. City planning of Edo: religion design of the architect group. Kodansha. (in

Japanese)

4) Suzuki, M., 2000. Edo was created in this way: restoration of a vision for one hundred years. Chikuma Shobo. (in Japanese)

5) Tokyo Machiaruki Iinkai, 2002. Excursion of Tokyo Seven Lucky Gods. NHK Publishing. (in Japanese)

6) Kikuchi, T., 2008. Learning of tourism; open with enjoying tourism. Ninomiya Shoten. (in Japanese)

7) Masai, Y., 2011. Deep understanding of Tokyo geography from history and map. Seisyun Publishing. (in Japanese)

8) Imao, K., 2016. Railway development history in Tokyo; elucidation with maps. JTB Publishing. (in Japanese)

9) Japanese Cabinet Office, 2019. Atlas of fire dynamics map (Report of Examination Prevention Committee) [http://www.bousai.go.jp/kyoiku/kyokun/kyoukunnokeishou/rep/1923_kanto_daishinsai/data/pages/20003.html] (accessed 13 November 2019)

10) Koshigawa, A., 1991. City planning of Tokyo. Iwanami Shoten. (in Japanese)

Close-up: Edo's spatial range

1) Suzuki, M., 2006. Geography and place names of Edo/Tokyo: a timeless walk from towns to the city. Nippon Jitsugyou Publishing. (in Japanese)

2) Naito, M., 2010. Downtown of Edo; Development of a megacity. Soshisha. (in Japanese)

3) Masai, Y., 2000. Maps and landscape of Edo/Tokyo; from a mega city to a global super city. Kokon Shoin. (in Japanese)

4) Iida, R. and Tawara, M., 1988. History of Edozu. Tsukiji Shokan. (in Japanese)

5) Yamaguchi, K., 1995. History of Ukiyo-e. Sanichi Shobo. (in Japanese)

Close-up: Edo's public holidays

1) Nishiyama, M., 1983. Collection of Nishiyama Matsunosuke works, vol. 3, Lifestyle and its culture in Edo. Yoshikawa Koubunkan. (in Japanese)

2) Arioka, T., 2007. Cultural history of human and goods, vol. 1, Japanese cherry. Hosei University press. (in Japanese)

3) Kubota, J., Tsutsumi, S. and Miyoshi, Y., 1990. New-compiled history of Japanese literature. Shogaku Tosho. (in Japanese)

Close-up: Tokyo's place names

1) Takemitsu, M., 1997. Encyclopedia of the origin of place name. Tokyodo Publishing. (in Japanese)

2) Tokyo Chuo City's Kyobashi Library (ed.), 1994. Historical maps of Chuo City, the part of Tsukushima area. Tokyo Chuo City Kyobashi Library. (in Japanese)

Close-up: Edo's food culture

1) Okubo, Y., 2012. Dining spaces in Edo: from stall food to Japanese cuisine. Kodansha. (in Japanese)

Chapter 6: Living in Tokyo

1) Ministry of Health, Labour and Welfare, 2018. 2018 list of regional minimum wages revision in Japan. (in Japanese)

2) Ministry of Land, Infrastructure, Transport and Tourism (eds.), 2018. White paper on Tokyo metropolitan area 2018. Shobi Printing. (in Japanese)

3) Wakabayashi, Y. and Koizumi, R., 2014. Spatial patterns of population change in the 23 wards of Tokyo after the period of the bubble economy. Journal of Geography (Chigaku Zasshi) 123, 249–268. (in Japanese)

Close-up: Tokyo's historic Shitamachi and Yamanote

1) Yamaguchi, H. (ed.), 1987. Pedigree of suburban residential area: rural utopia in Tokyo. Kajima Publishing. (in Japanese)

2) Matsuyama, M., 2014. Urban history of Edo/Tokyo: city, architecture and society in the development period of modern Japan. University of Tokyo Press. (in Japanese)

3) Tokyo Asahi News Paper, 1923. Den'en Toshi area sales. (27 November 1923 evening edition) (in Japanese)

Close-up: Revival of Tokyo's new towns
1) Sato, R. and Miyazawa, H.(eds), 2018. Modern human geography. Foundation for the Promotion of the Open University of Japan.

Close-up: Tokyo's islands
1) Konno, S., Nagano, T. and Nagahama, T., 1972. Industrial structure of Izu Kôzushima and its change. Tohoku Geography 24, 222-232. (in Japanese)
2) Ochiai, M., Kozawa, M., Sato, A. and Sato, M., 1982. The development of tourist industry and minshuku management at Niijima in Izu Islands. The Journal of Geography, Tokyo Gakugei University 36, 29-52. (in Japanese)

Close-up: Tokyo's subway system
1) Wakuda, Y., 1987. Subway sytems in Japan. Iwanami Shoten. (in Japanese)
2) Yajima, T. and Ieda, H. (eds.), 2014. Transit oriented development Tokyo, a global city created by railways. The Institute of Behavioral Sciences. (in Japanese)

Chapter 7: Tokyo's Economy
1) Fukui, K., 2016. The role of the IT programmer community in IT venture companies in Tokyo: an analysis of a major technology conference in Tokyo. Annals of the Association of Economic Geographers 62, 87-101. (in Japanese)
2) Yabe, N. 2005. Location analysis of software industries in the Tokyo metropolitan area: a nested logit model. Geographical Review of Japan 78, 514-533. (in Japanese)
3) Machimura, T., 1994. World city Tokyo's structural change: sociology of urban restructuring. University of Tokyo Press. (in Japanese)
4) Sassen, S., 2001. The global city: New York, London, Tokyo. Princeton University Press.
5) Hino, M. and Kagawa, T. (eds.), 2015. The changing Japanese metropolitan area under the post-growth society. Nakanishiya Publishing. (in Japanese)

Close-up: Ginza in Tokyo
1) Okamoto, S., 2006. Ginza 400 year's narrative: history of urban space. Kodansha. (in Japanese)

Close-up: Urban farming in Tokyo
1) Iizuka, R., Ota, K. and Kikuchi, T., 2019. Growth and sustaining strategies of urban agriculture based on interaction with urban residents: the case of Kodaira city, Tokyo metropolis. Journal of Geography (Chigaku Zasshi) 128, 171-187. (in Japanese)

Close-up: Harajuku backstreets and fashion
1) Yabe, N., 2018. Street fashion in Ura-Harajuku, factors in retail agglomeration, and effects on apparel production. In Kikuchi, T. (ed.), Geography of tourism: considering on regional attractions through tourism, 18-27, Ninomiya Shoten. (in Japanese)

Close-up: *Machi-kōba* in Tokyo
1) The Local Museum of Ota Ward (ed.), 1994. Explorative guide book; the history and development of industry in Ota Ward. The Local Museum of Ota Ward. (in Japanese)

Chapter 8: Tourism in Tokyo
1) Mizoo, Y., 2008. Theory of tourism resources; a consideration of classification systems. Josai International University Bulletin 16, 1-13. (in Japanese)
2) Sugimoto, K. and Kikuchi, T., 2014. Regional characteristics of the distribution of tourism resources in Japan. Journal of Geography (Chigaku Zasshi) 123, 1-24. (in Japanese)
3) Ministry of Internal Affairs and Communications, 2018. Administrative evaluation and monitoring on the use and management of recreational forests report. [http://www.soumu.go.jp/main_content/000590860.pdf] (last accessed 30 March 2019)
4) MICE International Competitiveness Enhancement Committee, 2015. Enhancing Japan's MICE international competitiveness: building an immovable position as the top international conference

host in Asia. Final Report of the MICE International Competitiveness Enhancement Committee. [http://www.mlit.go.jp/common/001169620.pdf] (last accessed 30 March 2019)

5) Tokyo Metropolitan Government, 2015. Tokyo MICE attracting strategy; aiming to establish a solid presence. [http://www.sangyo-rodo.metro.tokyo.jp/tourism/mice/pdf/150903honbun.pdf] (last accessed 30 March 2019)

Close-up: Two Tokyo Olympics

1) Oikawa, Y., 2009. Socio-economic history of the Tokyo Olympics. Nihon Keizai Hyoronsha. (in Japanese)

2) Tokyo Metropolitan Archives, 2018. Metropolitan history collection; Olympics and Tokyo, vol. 7. Tokyo Metropolitan Government, Division of the Bureau of Citizens and Cultural Affairs. (in Japanese)

3) Kataki, A., 2010. The Olympic city Tokyo 1940–1964. Kawade Shobo Shinsha. (in Japanese)

Close-up: Tower-based tourism in Tokyo

1) Kawamura, E., 2013. Cultural history of Towers. Maruzen Publishing. (in Japanese)

2) Edo Tokyo Museum (ed.), 2012. Special exhibition on the completion of Tokyo Skytree; the story of city and tower. Edo-Tokyo Museum. (in Japanese)

3) Tokyo Tower Official web page [http://www.tokyotower.co.jp/index.html] (last accessed 16 July 2015).

4) Tsugawa, Y., 2013. The role of tower as a landmark. Chiri 58 (6), 14–23. (in Japanese)

Close-up: Mt. Takao: Tokyo's most popular mountain

1) Takino, T., 1981. Tokyo park handbook 24, Visiting and investigation of Takao area. Kyogakusha. (in Japanese)

2) Michelin, 2015. The green guide Japan, 3rd ed. Michelin Travel Partner. (in Japanese)

Close-up: Ueno shopping streets and inbound tourism

1) Taito Ward Industrial Promotion Association, 2014.

2) Ota, K., Sugimoto, K., Kikuchi, T. and Doi, T., 2017. Spatial construction of commercial accumulation in the Ueno district, Tokyo. The International Journal of Tourism Science 10, 1–8. (in Japanese)

Conclusion: Future of Tokyo: Sustainable Tokyo

1) Kikuchi, T., 2011. Regional geography of Japan. Asakura Publishing. (in Japanese)

2) Domestic network-Headquarters and local stations [https://www.nhk.or.jp/corporateinfo/english/organizations_and_network/index.html] (last accessed 4 February 2020)

3) Kanno, M., Sano, M. and Taniuchi, T. (eds.), 2005. Regional geography of capital area I. Asakura Shoten. (in Japanese)

4) oneworld Interactive Network Map [http://onw.innosked.com] (last accessed 4 February 2020)

5) Suzuki, N., 2012. Why Tokyo is the best city in the world. PHP Institute. (in Japanese)

6) OECD, 2008 [http://www.oecd.org/science/inno/37569377.pdf] (last accessed 4 February 2020)

7) Kikuchi, T. and Sugai, T. (eds.), 2018. Tokyo as a global city, Springer.

8) Koshigawa, A., 2014. The legacy of city planning in Tokyo; prevention of disasters, rehabilitation and the Olympic Games. Chikuma Shobo. (in Japanese)

9) Cabinet Office, 2004. White Paper on Disaster Management 2004. National Printing Bureau. (in Japanese)

Index

編集者紹介

菊地俊夫 Toshio Kikuchi
東京都立大学都市環境科学研究科教授
Professor, Graduate School of Urban Environmental Sciences,
Tokyo Metropolitan University

松山　洋 Hiroshi Matsuyama
東京都立大学都市環境科学研究科教授
Professor, Graduate School of Urban Environmental Sciences,
Tokyo Metropolitan University

佐々木リディア Lidia Sasaki
東京都立大学国際センター特任准教授
Associate Professor, International Center,
Tokyo Metropolitan University

エランガ・ラナウィーラゲ Eranga Ranaweerage
東京都立大学都市環境科学研究科特任助教
Assistant Professor, Graduate School of Urban Environmental Sciences,
Tokyo Metropolitan University

Geography of Tokyo

定価はカバーに表示

2020 年 11 月 1 日　初版第 1 刷

編集者	菊　地　俊　夫
	松　山　　　洋
	佐々木リディア
	エランガ・ラナウィーラゲ
発行者	朝　倉　誠　造
発行所	株式会社 朝　倉　書　店

東京都新宿区新小川町 6-29
郵 便 番 号　162-8707
電　話　03（3260）0141
FAX　03（3260）0180
http://www.asakura.co.jp

〈検印省略〉

シナノ印刷・渡辺製本

© 2020 〈無断複写・転載を禁ず〉

ISBN 978-4-254-16362-9　C 3025　　　　Printed in Japan

JCOPY 〈出版者著作権管理機構 委託出版物〉
本書の無断複写は著作権法上での例外を除き禁じられています．複写される場合は，
そのつど事前に，出版者著作権管理機構（電話 03-5244-5088，FAX 03-5244-5089,
e-mail：info@jcopy.or.jp）の許諾を得てください．

Geography of Tokyo

日本語版 Japanese Edition

東京地理入門

―東京をあるく、みる、楽しむ―

菊地俊夫・松山 洋 ［編］

A5 判 160 頁 本体 2400 円＋税

ISBN 978-4-254-16361-2

【目次】

東京を見る／東京の地形／東京の気候／東京の動植物／東京の水と海／
東京の歴史と文化／東京に住む／東京の経済／東京の観光／東京の未来

東京の地理を自然地理・人文地理双方の視点から，最新の知見とともに
バランスよく解説。概説とコラムで東京の全体像を知る。

朝倉書店の英語書籍

Ordinary Differential Equations and Physical Phenomena

（『常微分方程式と物理現象』英語版）

by **Manabu Kanda** translated by **Alvin C. G. Varquez**

B5 判 160 頁 本体 3200 円＋税

ISBN 978-4-254-20169-7

The Japanese Language （英語で学ぶ日本語学）1

Japanese Linguistics （日本語学）

by **Mark Irwin and Matthew Zisk**

A5 判 304 頁 本体 4800 円＋税

ISBN 978-4-254-51681-4

上記価格（税別）は 2020 年 10 月現在